An Arrow in His Hand

Maria Vadia

Queenship

PUBLISHING COMPANY
P.O. Box 220 • Goleta, CA 93116
(800) 647-9882 • (805) 692-0043 • Fax: (805) 967-5133

Scripture Passages:

The Holy Bible, Ignatius Press, Revised Standard Version, Catholic Edition. Thomas Nelson and Sons, 1966.

Other Bibles used:

New American Bible, Saint Joseph Edition, Catholic Book Publishing Co. New York, 1970.

New King James Version, Spirit Filled Bible, 1991, Thomas Nelson, Inc.

The Message, The Bible in Contemporary Language. Peterson, Eugene H. Navpress 2002.

Concordance:

The New Strong's Exhaustive Concordance of the Bible. Strong, James, LL.D., S.T.D. 1995. Thomas Nelson Publishers.

———————————

Library of Congress Number # 2006920479

Published by:
    Queenship Publishing
    P.O. Box 220
    Goleta, CA 93116
    (800) 647-9882 • (805) 692-0043 • Fax: (805) 967-5133
    www.queenship.org

Printed in the United States of America

ISBN: 1-57918-295-X

I dedicate this book to our Lord and Savior, Jesus Christ, who is the "chief intercessor" at the right hand of our Father.

I thank Rene and Fifi, plus my sisters and brothers in the Lord who faithfully intercede for me and my family, especially my weekly intercessors: Mary, Mercedes, Niquin, Ina, Lucette, Cristina, Marina and Pilar. Without you I could not carry on with the Lord's work successfully! I love you!

W e're in a battle! As God's people, we need to rise up in the power of the Holy Spirit and fight the good fight of faith (2 Timothy 6:12). We need to enforce the victory of Calvary in every area of our lives. The battle is not against flesh and blood but against the unseen forces of darkness (Ephesians 6:12), who have already been defeated. We are seated "with Him in the heavenly places in Christ Jesus" (Ephesians 2:6), "far above all rule and authority and power and dominion" (Ephesians 1:21). Victory is ours! Our prophetic prayers of intercession can become "arrows" in the hand of our God in order to hit the target. We are God's representatives on earth; He expects us to pray His prayers and give birth to his plans and purposes for this hour. We are His army! All of us are called to intercede. With the help of our precious Holy Spirit, the Spirit of wisdom and revelation, we can search the heart of God and stand in the gap for the Church, nations, cities, governments, families, children, so that His will and purposes are accomplished. We know it's His will for "all men to be saved and to come to a knowledge of the truth." (Timothy 2:4). We must wage war against the forces of darkness that are keeping many in bondage, preventing them from coming to know the Truth, the Lord Jesus Christ.

The Lord says in Ezekiel 22:30:

" And I sought for a man among them who should build up the wall and stand in the breach before me for the land, that I should not destroy it; but I found none."

The Lord still searches today for a people He can partner with; a people that is willing to lay down their lives to intercede for His purposes. A people that will plead mercy and pray His prayers! Don't assume that He will do it without us! He won't! Let's not ignore today the need for intercession as in the days of Ezekiel!

"Like arrows in the hand of the warrior are the son's of one's youth. Happy is the man who has his quiver full of them!" (Psalm 127:4-5).

Allow the Lord our God, who is a "warrior" (Exodus 15:3), to put you in His quiver!

FOREWORD

By Rev. Raymond Skonezny, S.T.L., S.S.L.

Is there a person today who does not sense the crisis of a world torn by the deliberate choice of countless persons for whom God is at best a passing thought? The collapse of faith in Europe, the materialism and disintegration of the morality of persons and nations create the environment where evil is perceived as good and good perceived as evil. Is it any wonder that fear and anxiety escalate all around us?

Maria Vadia has brought to us a work that truly attacks the fear, emptiness, arrogance, and pride of modern man. She does so by bringing before us a cry not to flee the world but rather to face the enemy, clothed with the armor of God given to all of us who embrace the Lord. Of old, David (1 Sm. 17:40-47) slew the giant by entering the battle knowing that it was ultimately the battle of the Lord and he was the instrument.

In this work she brings before our eyes how the battle today is "not against flesh and blood but against the unseen forces of darkness". To fight this enemy she presents to us numerous passages of the Word of God and the role of the Holy Spirit. It is the Holy Spirit who opens our mind and hearts to face the world and bring Jesus, the Lord, to expel its darkness. It is by the Holy Spirit we speak the name of Jesus. It is by the Spirit we have the courage to lay down our lives to intercede in, with and through Christ for His followers, for His Church and the people of the world.

In this way we become as the title of the book proclaims "An Arrow in His Hand." Formed by the Word of God, called by Jesus into His intercessory death, resurrection and life before the Father, we fight the good fight of faith. We are called to enter into the Heart of The INTERCESSOR and become Christ's spiritual warriors to bring the "obedience of faith" into the world. "Repent and believe the good news" (Mk. 1:15) are the first words Jesus proclaims to the world after his return from the desert.

This slim volume challenges us to be both the arrow and the

arrow bearer to pierce the proud, arrogant, hardened heart of the cultures of death. Then the life-giving love of the Holy Spirit will enter and transform the face of the earth one person at a time. May the reader be empowered by the Spirit of the Living God to be like David before the modern-day Goliaths!

In conclusion, I highly recommend this book; and the spirit that breathes from every page is evident in the biblical passages effortlessly chosen to illustrate her points. Her final paragraph is a prayer that briefly sums up her hopes and desires for those who read and become the intercessors of today.

"Dear reader, my prayer is that there's a fire burning in your heart for more of God. As you seek His face, He will reward your efforts (Hebrews 11:6). It's His desire to draw you close and reveal His heart to you. It's His desire to change you into a 'first class warrior!' Your prayers of intercession are important! I pray that they rise before Him as sweet incense in His sight! It doesn't matter who you are, how old or how young, the color of your skin, what you do in life.... He's waiting for you to approach Him. As you hear, believe and proclaim, you will see His power and glory released! Amen."

To this prayer may all add their own Amen!

CONTENTS

I. INTERCESSION

A CALL FOR INTIMACY

"The friendship of the Lord is for those who fear Him, and He makes known to them His covenant." (Ps. 25:14).

"The secret of the Lord is with those who fear Him, and He will show them His covenant." (Ps.25:14). (NKJ).

As God's people, redeemed by His blood, we are a nation of "priests and kings" (1 Peter 2:9; Rev. 1:6; Rev. 5:10). Every child of God has an awesome "priestly" privilege (and responsibility) to go before the throne and minister to Him with our thanksgiving, praise and worship, adoration, prayers and intercessions. This is our first call; this is top priority. This is how a personal relationship with the Lord is developed and nurtured: spending time with Him daily. This is how a friendship is cultivated. This is how we fall in love with Jesus more and more. As this friendship and intimacy daevelops, the Lord promises to show us His covenant and we learn to recognize His voice. We transition from servants to friends:

"You are my friends if you do what I command you. No longer do I call you servants, for the servant does not know what his master is doing; but I have called you friends, for all that I have heard from my Father I have made known to you." (John 15:14-15).

When we are in right relationship with God and a friendship develops, the Holy Spirit will show us what the "master is doing." Jesus says that the Holy Spirit, the Spirit of truth, "will declare to you the things that are to come." (John 16:13).

Sadly enough, when God's people get "busy," the first thing that is dropped or shortened is the time spent with Him. This is tragic, because it's in that place of intimacy that we are changed and transformed; that's where we hear His voice and we receive His vision and guidance; that's from where His power and anointing flow. Our "priestly" role will affect our "kingly" role! No wonder the enemy tries hard to keep us away from spending time with the Lord!

It's interesting to note that the Great Commission was spoken in an atmosphere of worship:

"Then the eleven disciples went away into Galilee, to the mountain which Jesus had appointed for them. When they saw Him, they worshipped Him; but some doubted. And Jesus came and spoke to them, saying, 'All authority in heaven and on earth has been given to Me. Go, therefore and make disciples of all nations....'" (Matt. 28:16-19).

In Acts 13 (1-4) we see that the church in Antioch heard the voice of the Holy Spirit "while they were worshipping the Lord" (v.2), the Holy Spirit telling them to "Set apart for me Barnabas and Saul for the work to which I have called them." It was in an atmosphere of intimacy and worship that the Holy Spirit spoke.

There should be something in our gut, that like David we say:

"Show me Your ways, O Lord; Teach me Your paths. Lead me in Your truth and teach me, for You are the God of my salvation; on You I wait all the day." (Ps. 25:4). (NKJ).

The Apostle Paul prays for the church in Ephesus that "the God of our Lord Jesus Christ, the Father of glory, may give to you the spirit of wisdom and REVELATION.... (Ephesians 1:17). Each of us needs personal revelation from the Lord; revelation of His love, His grace, His goodness, His voice, His Word, His power, His glory, His mercy, His agenda, His heart! But to know Him and hear His heartbeat we must spend time with Him! I take my hat off to the saints that went before us; I thank God for them and their examples and for their personal sacrifices and the trails they opened. However, I've reached the point in my life that I want to hear the Lord myself and have His revelation released more and more personally. I'm not satisfied! Are you? I thank the Lord for everything He's done in my life, but there has to be more! There's a divine discontent and dissatisfaction and hunger in my gut for more of HIM!

As God's people we are all "prophetic." This means that by the power of the Holy Spirit we are all able to hear His voice. Look at what Peter proclaimed on the day of Pentecost, quoting from Joel's prophecy:

> "And in the last days it shall be, God declares, that I will pour out My Spirit upon all flesh, and your sons and daughters shall prophesy, and your young men shall see visions, and your old men shall dream dreams; yea, and on my menservants and maidservants in those days I will pour My Spirit; and they shall prophesy." (Acts 2:17-18).

What does prophesy mean? It simply means that we are able to hear His voice and communicate it. Dreams and visions are part of the package. The Apostle Paul says in 1 Corinthians 14:31 that we "can all prophesy...." Jesus Himself said in John 10:4 that His sheep "know His voice." Now, why is this important? Because hearing His voice is part of having a personal relationship with Him. In order to intercede prophetically, we need to hear His voice (and then speak out what He tells us). The Lord longs to speak to each one of us personally. There are things He wants to show us and words He wants us to hear. The prophet Amos says in Amos 3:7:

> "Surely the Lord God does nothing without revealing His secret to His Servants the prophets."

The prophet Amos did not go to seminary or have any "religious" training. He says in chapter 7:14-15 "I am no prophet, nor a prophet's son; but I am a herdsman, and a dresser of sycamore trees, and the Lord took me from following the flock...." In other words, he was a shepherd and a farmer. You could be a housewife, a secretary, a banker, an engineer, a fireman or a doctor; the Lord longs for you to seek His face and hear His voice. He's looking for surrendered hearts. He delights when we hunger and thirst for Him. The time spent with Him is the most precious and the most important. It's also the time where nobody else sees you! It's not a waste of time!

> "O God, thou are my God, I seek thee, my soul thirsts for thee; My flesh faints for thee, as in a dry and weary land where no water is." (Psalm 63:1).

Let's pray: "O Lord, we are desperate for You. We are hungry and thirsty for You and Your presence. We long to see Your face; we long to hear Your Voice. You are all we want; we want to know You better. We position ourselves in Your hands so that you can have Your way in us and through us. Holy Spirit draw us closer to Jesus, our Bridegroom King!
Amen!

JUST EXACTLY WHAT IS "INTERCESSION?"

"...let them now make intercession to the Lord of hosts...." (Jeremiah 27:18).

Intercession is prayer, even though not all prayer is intercession. Intercession means finding out His will and then asking Him to do it. Jesus Himself "lives to make intercession" for us, who draw near to God through Him (Hebrews 7:25). The Greek word used here for intercession is "entunchano". It means to fall in with, meet with in order to converse; to plead with a person on behalf of another. So when we intercede we go before the throne of God, (through the blood of Jesus), and we have a meeting with the Lord on behalf of someone else. This is exactly what Jesus is doing now for us; He is interceding for us at the right hand of the Father. Romans 8:34 says that Jesus:

"is at the right hand of God, who indeed intercedes for us."

It's important for us to know that this is the ministry that Jesus is presently undertaking on our behalf. Why is this important? Because He is the Head of the body (us); and we must be one with Him as He intercedes in heaven for us. He is the "high priest of our confession." (Hebrews 3: 1). We must intercede in agreement with His intercession to see that His will and purposes are carried out. We as Catholics believe in the intercession of the saints (in heaven). This is a good thing! However, it should not make us complacent when it comes to intercession. The "saints" down here on planet earth have to intercede also before the throne of God, because without our intercession God won't move and the enemy will keep on advancing! Don't think that God will do it without us. He himself has set it up in such a way that we are to partner with Him; we are "God's fellow workers" (1 Corinthians 3: 9). The Apostle Paul says in 1 Timothy 2:1-2:

"First of all, then, I urge that supplications, prayers, intercessions, and thanksgivings be made for all men, for kings and all who are in high positions, that we may lead a quiet and peaceable life, godly and respectful in every way."

We can say that the state of a nation is totally related to their intercession. Can we say that life in America is quiet and peaceable, godly and respectful in every way? I don't think so! It's up to us then, the people redeemed by the blood of the Lamb, to pray and intercede for all men, starting with those in places of authority. As our intercession goes before the throne of God, He will move accordingly down here.

True intercession comes from above, the Holy Spirit showing us what to pray for and how to pray for it. This means that we need intimacy with the Lord, as mentioned in the previous chapter. Intercession flows out of relationship and fellowship with our God. We need to set aside time and learn how to hear His voice and recognize the language of the Holy Spirit so that we can become "an arrow" in His hand as we prophesy, declare and proclaim His will for that situation. It's important that we speak out what He has shown us, for something is established in the Spirit realm when we do so. Isaiah says that the Lord:

"...confirms the word of his servant, and performs the counsel of his messengers...." (Isaiah 44:26).

The Hebrew word for intercession that is used frequently in the Old Testament is called "paga." It means to reach; to meet someone; to pressure or urge someone strongly; to assail with urgent petitions. It also means "falling upon" someone in battle, that is, to meet up with the enemy with hostile intent. This word for intercession is two-fold; it involves reaching God, meeting God, entreating Him for His favor and then coming against the enemy. I believe this word captures the essence of the fact that we are "priests and kings." We enter the presence of the Lord as "priests" to praise, worship and make intercession before we exercise our power and authority as "kings" over the enemy. The Apostle Paul tells us in Ephesians 6 to put on "the whole armor of God" because he knows that the spiritual battle is fought within the context of prayer. When we don't exercise this glorious privilege and responsibility, God is not pleased with us. Let me quote again Ezekiel 22:30:

> "And I sought for a man among them who should build up the wall and stand in the breach before me in the land, that I should not destroy it; but I found none."

Can you sense the frustration and pain in the Lord that He was not able to find even one person to come before Him and plead mercy for His people? One person would have been sufficient for Him not to destroy the land! Isaiah 59:14-15 says:

> "Justice is turned back, and righteousness stands far off; for truth has fallen in the public squares, and uprightness cannot enter. Truth is lacking, and he who departs from evil makes himself a prey. The Lord saw it, and it displeased Him that there was no justice. He saw that there was no man, and wondered that there was no one to intervene...."

In the days of Isaiah, as in the days of Ezekiel, there was evil and injustice in the land, a lack of truth and righteousness and the Lord "wondered" that no one intervened on behalf of the oppressed. "No one calls for justice, nor does any plead for truth. They trust in empty words and speak lies; they conceive evil and bring forth iniquity." (Isaiah 59:4). (NKJ).

Let me quote Ezekiel 13:3-5:

> "Thus says the Lord God, 'Woe to the foolish prophets who follow their own spirit, and have seen nothing! Your prophets have been like foxes among ruins, O Israel. You have not gone up into the breaches, or built up a wall for the house of Israel, that it might stand in battle in the day of the Lord.'"

The prophets or watchmen were supposed to 'see' and warn and protect God's people from the attacks of the enemy, but they were not doing their job. There were "seeing" nothing. Israel was left defenseless without a wall of protection. Does that sound familiar to us? Isn't it time that we as God's people arise and build walls and hedges of protection around our families, cities, nations and Church, who are in ruins?

As a mother of four, one of the things that I realized when I came to the Lord was the responsibility of interceding for my children. I pray and intercede for them daily, proclaiming and decreeing God's blessings over their lives, asking God for favor, building a hedge of protection around them, asking the Lord to release His angelic protection, etc., etc. Some years ago, my son Eddy went to a sailing race in the northeast. After the weekend race was over, Eddy asked around for a ride to the airport. He would be staying that night in the airport hotel, as his flight was leaving the next morning. A man "with long hair" who had been in the race volunteered to take my son to the airport. This man was very kind and patient with my son, as Eddy not only took a long time to get ready, but this man even drove him (in the opposite direction) back to the house to get his belongings. On the way to the airport the man suggested to Eddy that he didn't have to stay overnight in the hotel; that Eddy was welcome to stay with him. Eddy asked him (prompted by the Holy Spirit, I believe) what he did for a living. The man said that he made pornographic movies! Eddy had the courage to tell him to take him to the airport because "my mother wouldn't like that!" (He blamed it on me!) I believe this man thought that he had his next porno star sitting in his car. When my son shared with me what had happened, I couldn't thank the Lord enough that my child was alive and well. My mind went wild, thinking about all the missing persons, murders and rapes in this country! I also realized that the enemy has his "agents" released to come against the people of God. Now, when I intercede for my children, in the name of Jesus I cancel the enemy's plans against my children, "for no weapon that is fashioned against you shall prosper...." (Isaiah 54:17).

Recently my daughter had a prophetic dream in which she was tanning in South Beach. (South Beach is not the place where you want your children to be!) While she was lying on an extension chair getting sun, many snakes and serpents appeared and they were coming in her direction; she became scared. The snakes had different colors; orange, yellow, green, red. Suddenly, (in the dream), I showed up, fully equipped, and I started killing the snakes! Now, that's a great example of "paga" intercession! The snakes, of course, represent the evil spirits that the enemy had released against her. I was the one used by the Lord to keep the enemy from harming her through my intercession. The Lord revealed to her in a dream what was really taking place in the spiritual realm!

So intercession involves a relationship with the Lord that needs to be nurtured so that we can start hearing His voice more and more accurately in order to pray His prayers. It involves seeking His face, entering into His presence, worshiping Him, being sensitive to the Holy Spirit, being available and willing to be inconvenienced on behalf of someone else. It involves proclaiming, declaring, decreeing His will. It means to carry a "burden" placed in our heart by the Lord; it's birthed out of intimacy with Him. As we hear His voice or receive a vision, or He gives us a passage of Scripture, a song, a dream or a dance, we will have an "arrow" to shoot as we proclaim, declare and decree His will. That "arrow" will hit the target and the enemy will have to flee!

"He sent out His arrows and scattered the foe...." (Ps. 18:14).

BECOME MY WARRIORS,
NOT MY "WORRIERS"!

"Blessed be the Lord, my rock, who trains my hands for war, and my fingers for battle" (Ps. 144:1).

Worrying doesn't win any battles; it actually creates more stress and anxiety in our lives. It's basically a lack of trust in the Lord and a fruit of pride. We think the Lord can't handle it. It can become a stronghold in our minds where the enemy can send his darts to torment us and rob us of peace. I know this well because I was a first class worrier. Worry and anxiety can also produce deterioration in our bodies, such as ulcers and fatigue. The word of God clearly tells us not to worry:

"Therefore I tell you, do not be anxious about your life...." (Matthew 6:25).

"Cast all your anxieties on Him, for He cares about you." (1 Peter 5:7).

"Have no anxiety about anything...."   (Phillipians 4:6-7).

The Apostle Paul says not to worry or be anxious about ANYTHING!   Instead we release our concerns to the Lord, with thanksgiving, and His peace will guard our hearts and minds. An exchange needs to take place between the Lord and us: we give Him our worries and concerns, anything that causes us anxiety, and in return He gives us His peace! What a deal! Worrying and stressing out can become a real hindrance in listening to the voice of the Lord and taking action against the enemy. When Jesus visited Mary and Martha, he had to set Martha straight, because she was upset that Mary "sat at the Lord's feet and listened to His teaching," while she did all the work. From Martha's perspective, Mary was not "with it"; she should be helping with dinner! However, the Lord's perspective was quite different:

"Martha, Martha, you are anxious and troubled about many things; one thing is needful. Mary has chosen the good portion...." (Luke 10:41).

Martha was so anxious and worried that it cluttered her vision. She was unable to focus on what was really important; therefore, her choice was not the best one. She missed the opportunity to sit at the Lord's feet, the good portion! How often we do the same!

Years ago, I was worshiping the Lord in our prayer group and I heard His voice telling me to "become My warrior, not My worrier." How was this stronghold of worrying broken in my life? By spending time with the Lord in praise and worship and studying the Scriptures. Our perspective changes as we eat of His Word and we find out that the victory has already been won in Calvary. It's really a matter of enforcing what He has already won in Calvary. When we pray the Our Father, we are actually asking the Lord to bring down "heaven" into our circumstances. There's no worrying in heaven! We say "May your Kingdom come, may your will be done, on earth as it is in heaven." There's no lack in heaven! There are no tears, depression or sadness, sickness or disease in heaven! The kingdom of God is "righteousness and peace and joy in the Holy Spirit" (Romans 14:17). We are His representatives on this planet; the Apostle Paul says that "we are ambassadors for Christ" (2 Corinthians 5:20). In other words, we have full backing and provision to carry out the tasks the Lord has commissioned for us. There is no need to worry,

"for it is your Father's good pleasure to give you the kingdom." (Luke 12:32).

.

As we spend time with the Lord, He Himself will train us for battle against the enemy. He will show us that we need complete dependence on the Holy Spirit because it's "not by might, nor by power, but by My Spirit, says the Lord of Hosts." (Zechariah 4:6).

Let's pray: "Lord, I release every worry and concern that is keeping me burdened and anxious, and I place them in Your hands. From now on I choose instead to a trust you and not worry. Help me to wage war against the enemies of worry and anxiety that try to keep me from possessing Your promises. Help me to stay focused on You. Come, Holy Spirit, and help me now to rise up and exercise faith in this situation, to see His kingdom come and His will be done." Lord, change me into a first class WARRIOR!"

"He trains my hands for war, so that my arms can bend a bow of bronze." (2 Sam. 22:35).

OVERCOMING FEAR

"Now when they saw the boldness of Peter and John, and perceived that they were uneducated, common men, they wondered; and they recognized that they had been with Jesus." (Acts 4:13).

Fear is another enemy that we need to overcome so that we can intercede with confidence. Fear can keep us paralyzed and neutralized; and even worse, we will try to control. If you are fearful, I suggest that you do four things:

1. Spend time with Jesus! It's in His presence that we are changed into His likeness and transformed (2 Corinthians 3:17-18). Sing a new song to Him, praise Him, pray in tongues, sit still before Him. Praise releases the presence of God into our surrounding because it's our praises that He inhabits (Ps.22:3). As we behold the Lord Jesus, we are changed into His likeness. We become what we behold (2 Corinthians 3:18). Where the Spirit of the Lord is there is freedom! Freedom from what? From whatever is keeping us in bondage. In 2 Chronicles 20, when King Jehoshaphat was facing a battle with three enemy armies more powerful than his, he "feared, and set himself to seek the Lord...." (v.3). King Jehoshaphat did the right thing when he experienced fear: he sought the Lord. If you read the rest of the story, you'll find out how powerfully the Lord moved to give him the victory over his enemies. It was humanly impossible to win this battle; but with the Lord the impossible became reality! First step: seek His face! Usually we call everyone we know to tell them our tragedy. It's time to change our strategy! Call Him first! Give Him your "tragedy" and He'll give you His "strategy!" Our "911" is Jeremiah 33:3:

"Call to me and I will answer you, and will tell you great and hidden things which you have not known."

2. Spend time eating of His Word so that you can have a renewed mind and start thinking like He thinks (Romans 12:2). The

opposite of fear is faith, and faith comes by hearing, and hearing by the Word of God (Romans 10:17). Hundreds of times in the Bible the Lord tells us not to be afraid, as we're supposed to walk by faith and not by sight (2 Corinthians 5:7). Another important reason that we must walk by faith is this:

"And without faith it is impossible to please Him...." (Hebrews 11:6).

Jesus tried to train His disciples to overcome fear (not too successfully, I'm afraid; until they got baptized in the Holy Spirit!) in order to walk by faith. In Matthew 8:23-27, Jesus and His disciples are in a boat. A great storm comes against them:

"so that the boat was being swamped by the waves; but He was asleep. And they went and woke Him, saying, 'Save us, Lord; we are perishing.' And He said to them, 'Why are you afraid, O men of little faith?'"

Why did Jesus called them "men of little faith?" Because Jesus was expecting them to rise up and take authority over the winds and the sea themselves. That's exactly what He did and He was successful.

"Then He rose and rebuked the winds and the sea; and there was a great calm." (v.26).

The disciples "marveled, saying, 'What sort of man is this, that even winds and sea obey Him?'" The disciples received a new revelation of Jesus: that He was Lord of nature. There's a new revelation of His character in every storm! The storms of life and the attacks of the enemy are situations in which the Lord expects us to rise up and rebuke the enemy using His power and authority to do so (1 John 3:8), just as He did.

Here's another boat story. This time the disciples were alone in the boat while Jesus remained behind on land. The Bible says that Jesus "made the disciples get into the boat and go before Him to the other side...." (Matthew 15:22-33). Get this point across: Jesus made them get into the boat alone. In the first boat story Jesus was with them; the second time they're alone. They rowed and rowed for hours trying to get over to the other side but couldn't because the wind was against them and the boat "was beaten by the waves." Jesus showed up walking on the sea and they "cried for fear. But immediately he spoke to them, saying, 'Take heart, it is I; have no fear.'" Peter ventured out of the boat to walk on the sea and walked until he saw the wind and started to sink. When finally Jesus gets into the boat, "the wind ceased. And those in the boat worshiped Him saying, 'Truly you are the Son of God.'" This time the disciples received an even greater revelation: not only Jesus was Lord of nature, but the Son of God! This time they did more that marvel; they worshipped! Jesus was again training His disciples to walk by faith by keeping their eyes on Him and not on the circumstances.

"The wicked flee when no one pursues, but the righteous are bold as a lion." (Proverbs 28:1).

3.   Get filled with the Holy Spirit. You can do this as often as you like (Ephesians 5:18):

"for God did not give us a spirit of timidity but a spirit of power...." (2 Timothy 1:7).

How could Peter "suddenly" on the day of Pentecost become so fearless and bold to be able to preach to the multitude? Was it the result of a "How to Become a Better Speaker" seminar? Was it the result of a self-help book on public speaking? Of course not! It was the result of being filled with the Holy Spirit. Not only was he able to speak in front of the crowds that he had previously been afraid of, but he spoke prophetically, the Holy Spirit using his words as arrows to pierce the hearts of the listeners.

"Now when they heard this they were cut to the heart, and said to Peter and the rest of the apostles, Brethren, what shall we do?" (Acts 2:37).

15

In my own personal life my worst nightmare was to stand in front of a group a people to speak to them. During my university days, every time I was supposed to give an oral report in class, I would be scared, fearful and gripped by anxiety. I tried to get out of it by telling the teacher I would rather do three written reports than stand in front of the class. My point is that I dreaded to stand in front of people. The first time the Holy Spirit asked me to stand in front of the prayer group to speak, I said "no." When the Lord asked me the second time, I finally said "yes," with much fear and trembling. The Lord was training me right there in the prayer group, for in the future I would be speaking in front of many. I can testify that only by the power of the Holy Spirit have I been able to preach and teach God's people. That stronghold of fear had to be pulled down and destroyed by the Holy Spirit so that I could become who God had created me to be.

"The Lord is my light and my salvation; whom shall I fear? The Lord is the stronghold of my life; of whom shall I be afraid?" (Psalm 27:1).

4.   Tread over the spirit of fear (Luke 10:19).

I suggest that you stand up and start treading and stomping over that spirit of fear. The Lord wants to set you free. Start proclaiming with your mouth, out loud, 1 John 4:4, Luke 10:19, Acts 1:8, 2 Timothy 1:7. Remember, we have power in the tongue for death or for life (Proverbs 18:21); as you proclaim the Word of God you are releasing life into that situation. Pray in tongues for several minutes and ask the Lord to speak to you; it could be a vision, a sense in your spirit, a Word from Scripture, a song. Now, start proclaiming and shooting your "arrow." I remember a difficult time in my life when I was battling for my divorce settlement, and I was praying in tongues. As I was doing so, a Scripture passage came to my mind from Ps. 68:5-6,

"Father of the fatherless and protector of widows is God in His holy habitation. God gives the desolate a home to dwell in; He leads out the prisoners to prosperity...."

That passage became one of the "arrows" in my quiver. I sensed the Lord telling me that He was my father and my protector; that He would see to it that I would get a home and abundance. This Word has been fulfilled in my life! I still declare it as the Holy Spirit reminds me.

There are no quick fixes! This means you must make adjustments with your time. Maybe spend less time watching television and more time with the Lord!

OPEN MY EYES, LORD!

"Come up hither, and I will show you...." (Revelation 4:1).

The Lord wants to show us many things that are not visible to the natural eye. Why is this important? Because to intercede prophetically and hit the target we need to know certain things that are not visible to the natural eye. The Holy Spirit wants to show us what the Lord is doing so that we can cooperate with Him. There is a spiritual battle going on and the Holy Spirit wants to expose the strategies and the hidden snares of the enemy. The Holy Spirit might want to show us the root cause of a problem so that we can pray effectively, or He wants to bring revelation of destiny. As pilgrims in this world, we are not to "settle," but to keep moving forward. We need guidance, direction, confirmation and encouragement along the way. According to what the Lord told the church of Laodicea, the lukewarm church (Revelation 3:18), one of the things we need to "buy" to come out of lukewarmness is:

"salve to anoint your eyes, that you may see."

Jesus wept over Jerusalem because of the blindness and stubbornness of His people:

"And when He drew near and saw the city He wept over it, saying, 'Would that even today you knew the things that make for peace! But now they are hid from your eyes.'" (Luke 19:41-22).

When we refuse to see with our spiritual eyes, we will progressively become more and more blind and will not be able to "interpret the signs of the times" (Matthew 16:3). God's own people rejected the long awaited Messiah; one of the reasons was that He didn't come "packaged" in the way they expected. Jesus told them,

"...You did not know the time of your visitation." (Luke 19:44).

The Apostle Paul knew the importance of having our spiritual eyes opened; scales fell from his eyes after his encounter with Jesus! In the letter to the Ephesians he prays that our heavenly Father:

"may give you a spirit of wisdom and of revelation in the knowledge of Him, having the eyes of your hearts enlightened.... (Ephesians 1:17-18).

Peter, James and John saw Jesus transfigured right before their eyes, His face shining like the sun and His garments white as light (Matthew 17:1-8). They experienced His majesty and glory in that mountain. It was important for them to see Jesus in His glory, because soon they would see Jesus in His passion. Peter writes in 1Peter 1:16:

"For we did not follow cleverly devised myths when we made known to you the power and coming of our Lord Jesus Christ, but we were eyewitnesses of His majesty."

There is something about being "eyewitnesses"!

Isaiah's vision of the throne room of God totally changed him and his destiny (Isaiah 6). He saw the Lord "sitting upon a throne, high and lifted up...." In the presence of the Lord, the prophet realized his own sinfulness and said "for my eyes have seen the King, the Lord of hosts!" In the midst of all the corruption and apostasy in the land, Isaiah was able to know that the God of Israel was alive and well, sitting on His throne. Out of that encounter with the living God, Isaiah "volunteered" to be sent to God's people with the burden of the Lord. The Apostle John makes the point in his gospel that Isaiah "saw His glory and spoke of Him." (John 12:41).

In 2 Kings 6, the king of Syria sends his men to seize the prophet Elisha, because the prophet knows by the Spirit the king's plans and spoils them by telling them to his enemy, the King of Israel. Therefore, the king of Syria "sent there horses and chariots and a great army; and they came by night, and surrounded the city." When

Elisha's servant saw the enemy forces, he became afraid. Elisha told him:

> "Fear not, for those who are with us are more than those who are with them. Then Elisha prayed, and said, 'O Lord, I pray thee, open his eyes that he may see.' So the Lord opened the eyes of the young man, and he saw; and behold, the mountain was full of horses and chariots of fire round about Elisha."

Elisha and his servant were able to see into the spirit realm in a time of danger and know that "those who are with us are more than those who are with them." That changed their perspective! I believe we're living in times of great angelic activity and we are to know that the angels have been "sent forth to serve, for the sake of those who are to obtain salvation" (Hebrews 1:14). As the Lord opens our eyes more and more, I believe that many of us will be seeing the angels that have been released to help us as we carry on with the work of the Lord. This will be a great source of comfort.

As I intercede for people or pray with them, I always ask the Lord to show me what I need to know that I cannot see with my natural eyes, so that I can pray effectively. I ask the Lord for a word of knowledge or spiritual insight so that I can "hit the target." When we pray in tongues, we position ourselves for the Lord to show us what's in His heart. Recently a young man asked for prayer for physical healing. He had been feeling weak, had to be hospitalized and the doctors really didn't know what he had. As he kept explaining the symptoms, I sort of stopped listening to him and started to see what the Lord was showing me. The Lord showed me (in the Spirit), an older man, demanding and pointing with his finger. I had the sense that this was a picture of his father, who was a very demanding and hard man. I asked the young man if his father was like that. The young man responded "Was he ever demanding! If I walked into the house with a 'C' in my report he would go berserk." This was the root of the problem: his relationship with his father! We led the young man in a prayer of forgiveness for his father and prayed for inner healing. Immediately he started to feel better. Thank you, Jesus!

I believe the Lord wants to show us things before they happen. He wants us to be prepared and ready to labor with Him in prayer and intercession. The work of evangelization needs to be backed by intercession; He wants to show us things in the Spirit ahead of time so that we can pray effectively for a harvest of souls. Intercession for those in the frontlines is also necessary, as the enemy tries to sabotage the Lord's work in any way he can. I remember that just before my first trip to Africa, I was in Trinidad, and my friend Bernadette Patrick "saw" in the Spirit that I would need protection for my feet. She felt that the enemy would attack my feet. With that word in my heart, I was prepared for the streets in Ghana. I was very careful to watch where I was stepping; the roads were very uneven, full of holes and very little light at night. However, another sister in the Lord got injured as she kept twisting her ankle because of the holes in the street. I then gave her the Word that was given to me. In Isaiah 46:9-10 He says,

> "…for I am God, and there is no other; I am God, and there is none like Me, declaring the end from the beginning and from ancient times things not yet done, saying, My counsel shall stand, and I will accomplish all my purpose...."

The Lord wants to show us the end from the beginning; He gives us glimpses of the finished product so that we don't lose hope. Dreams and visions that have to do with our destiny in Christ can be great sources of encouragement and direction. When I first came to Christ, the Lord kept showing me a big map of the USA, with big, flashing light bulbs all around it. The Lord was showing me that one day I would go all around this country preaching and proclaiming the Gospel. Before that became a reality, however, I went through very difficult times. During one of those times, the Lord gave a dream to the housekeeper of a friend of mine, which helped me to stay on God's track. In the dream, she saw me carrying a backpack and going around the world doing the Lord's work. At a very difficult moment in my life, the Lord communicated that

I would be going to the nations! He gave my friend a dream to confirm and encourage me! And it came when I needed it the most! Thank you, Jesus!

On the Feast of the Immaculate Conception in 2005, I decided to stay praying after Mass. I was praying in tongues and suddenly I was in the spirit and I saw myself in a huge stadium preaching and people were getting healed right and left. I was totally amazed at what I saw! It was so unexpected! I told the Lord that He could do with me whatever He wanted; I just wanted confirmation of what I had seen. When I got home, there was a letter in the mail from a lady in San Antonio with whom I had prayed with for healing of cancer. She wrote in the letter that indeed the Lord had healed her! Thank you, Jesus! Why is this important for me? Because I know that the Lord wants me to pray for the sick and this is one thing that my friends can intercede for as I go forth with the work of the Lord. Amen!

A friend of mine asked some of her friends to pray for her son, who was going through a time of great emotional and mental turmoil. The Lord gave me a vision of this young man as a lifeguard, rescuing those who were in danger of drowning. The Lord showed me that after the struggle was over, He would use him to rescue and deliver many who were drowning in hopelessness and depression. It was a good word, since it was obvious that her son would come out victoriously from that season in his life. I used that word as an arrow of victory, proclaiming the end before we saw it. The Lord gave a dream to another friend in which she saw our friend's son being affirmed and encouraged by a middle-aged, bald man. This man turned out to be a real blessing in this young man's life; guiding, mentoring and connecting him into his destiny. Do you see how important are the prophetic gifts of the Spirit to comfort and encourage? (1 Corinthians 14:3). Amen!

In my last trip to Uganda, Africa, the Lord showed me things that He wanted to do before they happened. For example, He showed me a woman with a crooked leg that He wanted to heal. I started to pray for this lady even before I saw her. In the service that night I called for the woman to come up to the stage; she came, got prayed for, and was healed. She had been in an accident many years ago and her leg was crooked. She had been to many doctors but no healing. That night the Holy Spirit healed and straightened out her leg. What was really awesome was that I was able to see it before it happened and was able to pray beforehand for her. Thank you, Jesus!

> "Ask the Lord to show you new and hidden things so that you can become a more effective prayer warrior!" (Jeremiah 33:3).

> "It is the glory of God to conceal things, but the glory of kings is to search things out." (Proverbs 25:2).

OPEN MY EARS, LORD!

"Behold, I stand at the door and knock; if any one hears my voice and opens the door, I will come in to him and eat with him and he with me." (Revelation 3:20).

This verse from the Scriptures is not for unbelievers, but for believers; it was addressed to the Church of Laodicea, which had become lukewarm. We see the longing of the Lord for intimacy with His people. I imagine that the Laodiceans went to church regularly, but they were more like "pew potatoes," just sitting there until the service was over and then going back home to their regular routines. No relationship, no intimacy with the Lord, no change, no transformation, no hunger nor thirst for Jesus. They were more like spectators. In His mercy and because He loves us, He still knocks at the door of our hearts; but before we can open the door, we have to hear His knocks in order to open. Psalm 95:7(b)-8 says,

"O that today you would hearken to His voice! Harden not your hearts...."

There is a connection between lukewarmness and hardness of heart and spiritual deafness. If Jesus is not the center of our lives, if He's not our passion, if He's not our desire, we are becoming lukewarm and will end up with a hardened heart. It's a process; it doesn't happen overnight. We will fit into this category:

"You shall indeed hear but never understand... For this people's heart has grown dull, and their ears are heavy of hearing...." (Matthew 13:14-15).

Jesus is our Bridegroom King and He's in love with us, His Bride! He longs for us to hear His voice. In the Song of Solomon 2:8, the Shulamite says,

"The voice of my beloved! Behold, he comes, leaping upon the mountains, bounding over the hills."

She was able to recognize the voice of her beloved! Mary Magdalene didn't recognize the Risen Lord until He called her by name. Something happened inside Mary Magdalene when Jesus said her name; at that instant, she recognized Him! Jesus said in John 10:3 – 4,

"...the sheep hear His voice, and He calls His own sheep by name...."

"...the sheep follow Him for they know His voice."

If you are His sheep you can hear His voice! The Lord is looking for a people that long to hear His voice and are able to respond to it right away because they know it's Him.

"Sacrifice and offering thou dost not desire; but thou hast given me an open ear." (Psalm 40:6).

In 1992, during one of the lowest points in my life, just after the breakup of my marriage and the experience of financial disaster, I was sitting in front of the Blessed Sacrament and I heard the voice of the Lord. This is what I heard: "Write about the simple mysteries." I was perplexed; what was this about the "simple mysteries?" The Lord asking me to write, when I never liked writing? I just couldn't understand why at this time He would say such a thing! I would have rather heard something more comforting! I knew that priests during Mass said something about the "sacred mysteries" but this was something different. However, I stored that "word" in my heart and put it in the back burner. Later that year I accompanied Sr. Linda Koontz to Jamaica, where many people came to the Lord. One young Muslim who gave his life to Jesus gave me a gift just before we left Jamaica: a pen! I realized that the Lord was confirming and reminding me of what He had told me previously. I also realized that the "simple mysteries" are the secrets of the Kingdom, revealed to those that have their spiritual ears opened to the Truth. Jesus said in Luke 8:10, "To you it has been given to know the secrets of the kingdom of God...." This book you have in your hands is my third book! Somewhere along my walk with the Lord I dared to believe the word He had spoken to me. I share this story, because sometimes when we hear the voice of the Lord we don't understand right away; it seems almost ridiculous! But as you keep that word in your heart (Luke 2:51) and you keep watering the soil by "calling the things that are not as though they were" (Romans 4:17), the Holy Spirit will take that word and bring it to pass, to the glory of God! We have to be like Samuel, who

"...let none of His words fall to the ground." (1 Samuel 3:21).

I was married once, and every time my husband phoned me, I knew right away it was him. He didn't have to identify himself for I knew his voice. This is what the Lord wants; an intimate relationship where we are able to identify His voice. It's important that we know the voice of the Lord, because we hear three voices: the devil's, our own and the Holy Spirit's. Anything that doesn't conform to the written Word of God, we can discard. However, there are times that we need a specific word (in order to intercede successfully), and the answer is not in the Bible. Let me give you an example. A person knows he or she is called to the nations, and doesn't know if it's China or Africa; there are open doors for both nations and the person needs to make a decision. Another example: a person has two job offerings and doesn't know which one to take. Because we don't walk by sight, but by faith, we need to hear His voice in order to make the choices that please Him.

We're living in a time and season in which the Holy Spirit is doing a new thing and He wants to tell us. The thing is, the Holy Spirit is always on the move! Let's ask Him to unplug our ears so that we can hear His voice. This will help us to intercede successfully. Isaiah 42: 9 says,

"Behold, the former things have come to pass, and new things I now declare; before they spring forth I tell you of them."

Isaiah 48:6-7 says,

> "You have heard; now see all this; and will you not declare it? From this time forth I make you hear new things, hidden things which you have not known. They are created now, not long ago; before today you have never heard of them, lest you should say, behold, I knew them."

When we become "comfortable" with the ways of the Lord, there might be a tendency in many of us to resist the "new" things that He wants to do. But in this passage of Scripture the Lord says clearly that there are "new things" that are "created now" that He wants to show us for us to declare. The Holy Spirit is very creative. Every time that we intercede we should expect the Lord to show us the "new things" that He is doing so that we can declare them as "arrows" that will bring forth the victory.

Look at Isaiah 45:11 (NKJ):

> "Thus says the Lord, The Holy One of Israel, and His maker; ask Me of things to come, concerning My sons; and concerning the work of My hands, you command me."

This is absolutely amazing, that the God of the universe invites us to ask Him, even to demand of Him answers to the questions we have concerning "His sons" and the work of His hands. I looked up the word "ask" in the Hebrew dictionary and it is more than just asking nicely; it implies insistent and demanding asking. For some reason the Lord just loves for us to humbly come before Him with expectant faith knowing that we will hear His voice! As I meditate on all this verses of Scriptures, I know that there is so much more intimacy and fellowship that the Lord longs to have with us, His children. I also know that as His people, we are limiting His power today just as in days of old because of our lack of intercession.

Psalm 29:3 says that:

"The voice of the Lord is upon the waters...."

The challenge is for the waters, the "rivers of living water," which is the Holy Spirit, be released in us, through us, all around us! One way to open the "wells of salvation" (Isaiah 12:3) is by praising the Lord. We enter His gates with thanksgiving and His courts with praise (Psalm 100:4). Another way to get the rivers flowing out of the wells is through praying in tongues, the language of the Holy Spirit. As the waters start to flow, you will experience a change in the atmosphere. Freedom, joy, rejoicing, the voice of the Lord will start flowing. There, in the river, He will speak to us, guide us, show us what we need to know.

Seven times in the book of Revelation the Lord says to the seven churches:

"He who has an ear, let him hear what the Spirit says to the churches." (Revelation 2:7, 11, 17, 29; 3:6, 13, 22).

It's our responsibility to have "open" ears. We need to hear what the Holy Spirit is saying in order to move forward. There are changes and adjustments we need to make; strongholds that need to be pulled down in order to overcome. We are His Bride and we're supposed "to walk in the same way in which He walked" (1 John 2:6). Jesus walked in a constant communion with the Father, hearing His voice and obeying it. Amen!

"Has the Lord as great delight in burnt offerings and sacrifices, as in obeying the voice of the Lord? Behold to obey is better than sacrifice, and to hearken than the fat of rams." (1 Samuel 16:22).

SHOOT YOUR ARROWS!

"He made my mouth like a sharp sword, in the shadow of His hand He hid me; He made me a polished arrow, in His quiver He hid me away." (Isaiah 49: 2).

Faith has a voice. In order to intercede prophetically (shoot our arrows), we need to speak out, sing, proclaim, act out, what the Lord has shown us. Making declarations and decreeing God's will into a situation is necessary. There's power in our tongue for death and life (Proverbs 18:21), and as we declare what the Lord is doing we are bringing His will and purpose into that situation. What we see or what we hear, needs to be spoken to hit the target. Jesus released His authority by speaking out His commands against the winds, the waves, the enemy; He even spoke to a fig tree! (Mark 11: 14). Matthew says:

"He cast out the spirits with a word...." (Matthew 8:16).

Look at the need of speaking into a situation. Isaiah 42: 22 says,

"But this is a people robbed and plundered, they are all of them trapped in holes and hidden in prisons; they have become a prey with none to rescue, a spoil with none to say, Restore!"

This is a picture of a people in bondage, robbed, imprisoned, trapped. Not only that, they couldn't even defend themselves against the enemy and they had "none to rescue" and "none to say Restore!" It seems to me things haven't changed that much; but one thing we can change is our response! Isn't it time that we start interceding and speaking "Restoration!" to the ruins in our lives? The Apostle Paul says in 1 Corinthians 4: 13,

"Since we have the same spirit of faith as he had who wrote I believed, and so I spoke, we too believe, and so we speak."

As Jesus hung on the Cross, interceding on our behalf (Isaiah 53: 12b), I'm glad that He didn't just think about our forgiveness, but He spoke it out (Luke 23: 34). When He saw His mother and John, He just didn't think about their relationship with each other and the fact that we would need her as a mother, but He spoke it out. He said to His mother,

"Woman, behold your son!" (John 19:26).

He said to John,

"Behold your mother!" (John 19:27).

Intercession is not just a "mind" and "heart" thing; it's also a "mouth" thing. What you believe in your heart must be confessed with your mouth (Romans 10:9). In this way the Lord

"...confirms the word of His servant, and performs the counsel of His messengers." (Isaiah 44:26).

Psalm 32:8 says,

"I will instruct you and teach you the way you should go...."

The word "teach" in Hebrew, "yarah," not only means to instruct, but has several meanings: to direct, to point, shoot, aim, throw, cast in a straight manner. The Lord Himself will help us direct, point, aim, shoot our arrows of intercession!

In Joshua 10, Joshua spoke to the sun in the middle of a battle, commanding it to be still. He said in the sight of Israel,

"Sun, stand thou still at Gibeon, and thou Moon in the valley of Aijalon. And the sun stood still, and the moon stayed, until the nation took vengeance on their enemies.... The sun stayed in the midst of heaven, and did not hasten to go down for about a whole day. There has been no day like it before or since, when the Lord hearkened to the voice of a man; for the Lord fought for Israel." (Joshua 10: 12-14).

Joshua walked by faith; he spoke out what the Lord put in his heart and a miracle took place. His "arrows" commanding the sun to stand still hit the target! Look at what the prophet Habakkuk said thousands of years later:

"The sun and moon stood still in their habitation at the light of thine arrows as they sped, at the flash of thy glittering spear." (Habakkuk 3:11).

THE ENEMY SHOOTS ARROWS TOO!

"Hear my voice, O God, in my complaint; preserve my life from dread of the enemy, hide me from the secret plots of the wicked, from the scheming of evildoers, who whet their tongues like swords, who aim bitter words like arrows, shooting from ambush at the blameless, shooting at him suddenly and without fear. They hold fast to their evil purpose; they talk of laying snares secretly thinking, who can see us?" (Psalm 64: 1-5).

As we can see from this passage of Scripture, the enemy also uses people to shoot his arrows; they "aim their bitter words like arrows" and also "hold fast to their evil purpose." The enemy's arrows are "bitter words;" words of lies, deception and accusation. That's a ministry of the devil. Jesus calls him a liar and the father of all lies (John 8:44). He is a master at accusation; he's called "the accuser of our brethren... who accuses them day and night before our God." (Revelation 12:10). We must remember that there is power in our tongue, for life or for death (Proverbs 18:21). Words have power whether we like or not! I believe that's why the Apostle Paul tells us to:

"take up all God's armour, or you will not be able to put up any resistance on the evil day or stand your ground even though you exert yourselves to the full." (Ephesians 6: 13). (NJB).

Part of this armour includes the shield of faith; he says "take up all" of God's armour. He says,

"always carrying the shield of faith so that you can use it to quench the burning arrows of the evil one." (v. 16) (NAB).

The spiritual battle has a lot to do with "words." We need to be ready "always" to protect ourselves from the "burning arrows" of accusation, deception and lies which the enemy sends our way to torment us and discourage us. Look at what Psalm 11: 2 says,

"for lo, the wicked bend the bow, they have fitted their arrow to the string, to shoot in the dark at the upright in heart...."

Our perfect model is Jesus in the desert, when the enemy came to tempt Him, torment Him and harass Him in order to take Him out of His destiny (Matthew 4:1-11). How did Jesus respond? In faith! He was able to stand firm without wavering, protected by His shield, which enabled Him to use the Sword of the Spirit (the Word of God) effectively against the enemy. Notice that He did not remain silent, but He spoke the Word!

In Psalm 58, David cries out to God asking Him for help against the wicked:

"Their poison is like the poison of a serpent.... Break their teeth in their mouth, O God! Break out the fangs of the young lions, O Lord! ...When he bends his bow, let his arrows be as if cut in pieces." (vv.4-7) (NKJ).

David knew the power in the words of the wicked. He writes in Psalm 52: 2-4:

"Your tongue is like a sharp razor, you worker of treachery. You love evil more than good, and lying more than speaking the truth. You love all words that devour, O deceitful tongue."

Psalm 11:2 says,

"for lo, the wicked bend the bow, they have fitted their arrow to the string, to shoot in the dark at the upright in heart...."

Spiritual warfare is real!

It's worth taking a look at the prophet Elijah's response to queen Jezebel's threat. In 1 Kings 18, Elijah wins an amazing victory over the false prophets of Israel; "four hundred and fifty prophets of Baal and the four hundred prophets of Asherah, who eat at Jezebel's table." (v.19). After the victory, Ahab told Jezebel all that Elijah had done, and how he had slain all the prophets with the sword. Then Jezebel sent a messenger to Elijah, saying,

"So may the gods do to me and more also, if I do not make your life as the life of one of them by this time tomorrow." (1 Kings 19:1-2).

Elijah responded in an unexpected manner:

"Then he was afraid, and he arose and went for his life...." (v.3).

This man, who had just defeated eight hundred and fifty prophets by himself, was now running for his life because of the threat of one woman! What in the world happened to Elijah? Couldn't the same God that empowered him against all those false prophets, help him now deal with one woman? Not only that, he asked God,

"that he might die, saying, It is enough; now, O, Lord, take away my life...." (v.4).

Elijah apparently fell into a pit of despair, confusion, discouragement, depression and self-pity, to the point that he wanted to die; all because of the threat of Jezebel! The words of Jezebel were enough to put Elijah on the run! I don't have the complete answer, but it's obvious that her words were like "poisonous arrows" packed with fear and intimidation. She was a false prophetess who dealt in witchcraft and had a controlling spirit. Maybe Elijah took his "armour" off after his big victory, was left unprotected, and Jezebel's arrows hit the target. Could the same thing have happened to John the Baptist when he was in prison and became confused as to whether Jesus was the Messiah or not? Remember, Herodias "had a grudge against him and wanted to kill him...." (Mark 6: 19). Food for thought!

Another example of the power in the words of the enemy is found in 1 Samuel 17, where the giant Goliath is intimidating the entire army of Israel. Every day for forty days, "morning and evening," he would stand and shout "arrows" of intimidation and fear against them.

"When Saul and all Israel heard these words of the Philistine, they were dismayed and greatly afraid." (v.11).

One man was able to maintain the entire army of Israel gripped and paralyzed by fear, until David showed up!

The hatred of the devil was released in words also against Jesus as He hung in the Cross, to tempt Him out of the Father's perfect will and plan. Let's look at the gospel of Matthew, chapter 27: 39 -44:

" And those who passed by deriding him, wagging their heads and saying, 'You who would destroy the temple and build it in three days, save yourself! If you are the Son of God, come down from the cross.' So also the chief priests with the scribes and elders, mocked him, saying, 'He saved others; He cannot save himself. He is the King of Israel; let him come down now from the cross, and we will believe in him. He trusts in God; let God deliver him now, if he desires him; for he said, I am the Son of God.' And the robbers who were crucified with him also reviled him in the same way."

The enemy shot arrows to mock Him, torment Him, taunt Him and even tempt Him to "come down from the Cross" so that people would "believe." Thank God it didn't work!

"You will not fear the terror of the night, nor the arrow that flies by day...." (Psalm 91:5).

II. THE HEART OF AN INTERCESSOR

CULTIVATE A PURE HEART!

" ...but the upright are in his confidence." (Proverbs 3: 32).

The Lord has to find us faithful and true in order to trust us with revelation. There are "mysteries" in the kingdom, insight, wisdom, knowledge, secrets, that He wants to reveal to us as we "grow in the grace and knowledge of our Lord and Savior Jesus Christ." (2 Peter 3:18). He wants to use us in ever-increasing ways!

"Blessed are the pure in heart, for they shall see God." (Matthew 5:8).

. When Jesus becomes our passion and there is a desire in our hearts to see His purposes, His plans, His glory manifested in "the land of the living," He will start confiding in us by speaking to us and showing us new things.

In Numbers 12:3 it says that Moses "was very meek, more than all men that were on the face of the earth." Hebrews 11: 25-26 says that Moses chose "rather to share ill-treatment with the people of God than to enjoy the fleeting pleasures of sin. He considered abuse suffered for the Christ greater wealth than the treasures of Egypt...." Wow! No wonder he could be used of God so mightily! He left "everything" for God! That is why the Lord told Miriam and Aaron "...he is entrusted with all my house." (Numbers 12: 7). God was able to trust Moses "with all His house!" As you know, Moses was not only a deliverer, but also a mighty prophet:

"And there has not arisen a prophet since in Israel like Moses, whom the Lord knew face to face, none like him for all the signs and wonders which the Lord sent him to do in the land of Egypt...." (Deuteronomy 34:10-11).

Joseph, Jacob's son, who is a type of Christ, foreshadowing the

Messiah, was used by God powerfully to preserve God's people from extinction by famine. The Lord gave him great ability to interpret dreams. Under great temptation to sexual sin, he was able to overcome. His boss's wife kept trying to seduce him, but he was able to remain steadfast and faithful to the Lord.

> "...his master's wife cast her eyes upon Joseph, and said, Lie with me.... But he refused and said to his master's wife, 'Lo, having me my master has no concern about anything in the house, and he has put everything that he has in my hand; he is not greater in this house than I am; nor has he kept back anything from me except yourself, because you are his wife; how then can I do this great wickedness, and sin against God?' And although she spoke to Joseph day after day, he would not listen to her, to lie with her or to be with her." (Genesis 39: 7-10).

Joseph was faithful to the Lord even in private. He was faithful not to indulge (in the wrong things), even when it was freely offered to him. He maintained a pure heart and was able to "withstand in the evil day...." (Ephesians 6: 13). At the right time he was catapulted into his "destiny," a place of great authority! God was able to trust him with great favor!

Daniel, whom the Lord also used powerfully by entrusting him with great revelation to interpret dreams and with knowledge of future events, was determined not to be "contaminated" with what the world had to offer.

> "But Daniel resolved that he would not defile himself with the king's rich food, or with the wine which he drank; therefore he asked the chief of the eunuchs to allow him not to defile himself. And God gave Daniel favor and compassion...." (Daniel 1: 8-9).

Daniel made a resolution to keep a pure heart and God was able to trust him. The favor of God rested upon him and he did not abuse it.

Whom did the Lord use to go and minister to Saul of Tarsus after Saul had his encounter with Jesus? A "disciple" of Jesus called Ananias (Acts 9:10),

> "Now there was a certain disciple at Damascus named Ananias; and to him the Lord said in a vision, 'Ananias.' And he said, 'Here I am, Lord.'"

A disciple is more than just a church "member." It is someone who has left everything to follow Jesus. Ananias made himself available to His master; the Lord was able to trust him with the commission to go and minister to a man that had done "much harm" to His people in Jerusalem. Ananias trusted the Lord and the Lord trusted in him.

Having shown you something about the hearts of some of the saints that the Lord was able to trust and use so powerfully, how can I skip the Virgin Mary? Our Heavenly Father entrusted this young lady with His most precious promise and His most important plan of all eternity! Obviously, Mary was found trustworthy and faithful for God to trust her with so much. "Do not be afraid, Mary, for you have found favor with God." (Luke 1: 30). Luke 8:18 says,

> "Take heed then how you hear; for to him who has will more be given...."

We must conclude then that if Mary was entrusted to conceive, carry, deliver and nurture the Son of God, she had been heeding the word of God all along. She had been found faithful and trustworthy to bring the Savior into this world! She is also a beautiful picture of the prophetic. The Word of God came through the angel Gabriel and the Holy Spirit overshadowed her. The Word of God and the Holy Spirit together form an explosion of life and power. That's how God created the world (Genesis 1: 1-2) and that is also how we get "pregnant" with the plans and purposes of God.

> "And behold you will conceive in your womb and bear a son,

and you shall call His name Jesus…. The Holy Spirit will come upon you, and the power of the Most High will overshadow you…." (Luke 1:31-35).

She was a surrendered vessel in the hand of God. She considered herself "the handmaid of the Lord."

"Behold, I am the handmaid of the Lord; let it be to me according to your word." (Luke 1:38).

That meaning of the word handmaid is more like the understanding we have of the word "slave". So we see that Mary was living for God, docile to the Holy Spirit and ready to say "yes" to God's plan and purpose.

"Who shall ascend the hill of the Lord? And who shall stand in His holy place? He who has clean hands and a pure heart, who does not lift up his soul to what is false, and does not swear deceitfully. He will receive blessing from the Lord, and vindication from the God of his salvation." (Psalm 24: 4-5).

LIKE A CHILD!

"At that time Jesus declared, I thank thee, Father, Lord of heaven and earth, that thou has hidden these things from the wise and understanding and revealed them to babes; yea, Father, for such was thy gracious will." (Matthew 11:25-26).

The Lord delights in childlike simplicity and trust. This means that we believe like a child without having to analyze everything a hundred times. We act on what He says and not on what we think. We take Him at His word. Children are needy and dependent on their parents; they also need to grow. In the same way, we must remain humble and teachable, dependent on the Holy Spirit for everything, knowing our need for continual growth.

"Blessed is the man whose strength is in You, whose heart is set on pilgrimage." (Psalm 84:5). (NKJ).

The childlike, humble person knows that there is a continual need for more growth; after all, we are to advance the kingdom of God and take back the land the enemy has stolen. We can't settle and remain comfortable, but rather keep pressing on in the Spirit. We are really a tribe of pioneers, going forward into "uncharted territory." God forbid that we ever develop the "I've been there and done that" attitude that keeps us contented and satisfied from moving forward in the Lord! If we think we know it all, we shut ourselves off from fresh revelation from the Lord.

So in order to receive revelation from God we need to cultivate a child-like simplicity, teachable and open to the Holy Spirit. Everywhere Jesus ministered, there were basically two responses: the "babes" who readily believed, and the wise and learned who trusted in themselves and rejected Him. We need the Holy Spirit even to understand that Jesus is Lord! (1 Corinthians 12: 3). The Apostle Paul says,

"But the natural man does not receive the things of the Spirit of God, for they are foolishness to him; nor can he know them, because they are spiritually discerned." (1 Corinthians 2: 14). (NKJ).

The "wise men" from the East came to Jerusalem wanting to see the king of the Jews. Naturally, they went to the capital city, thinking that they would find the king in a palace. (That's where kings are usually born). However, after being informed, they journeyed to Bethlehem in search of the king,

> "and going into the house they saw the child with Mary his mother, and they fell down and worshiped him." (Matthew 2:11).

These "wise men" recognized that Jesus was king "when they saw the child with Mary," even though nothing in the physical realm pointed to it. It was hardly the setting of "royalty"! In contrast to the humility of the wise men, the chief priests and the scribes didn't even bother to check out the birth of Messiah. They were the ones that knew the prophetic word! They were the ones that gave the information regarding Messiah's birth to Herod!

It took revelation by the Holy Spirit for Elizabeth to recognize Mary as "the mother of my Lord." Elizabeth had just experienced herself the power of God in her old age. Somehow, when we have an experience of His power, we open more to the Holy Spirit and it becomes easier to believe like a child.

> "And when Elizabeth heard the greeting of Mary, the babe leaped in her womb; and Elizabeth was filled with the Holy Spirit and she exclaimed with a loud cry, 'Blessed are you among women, and blessed is the fruit of your womb! And why is this granted me, the mother of my Lord should come to me? For behold, when the voice of your greeting came to my ears, the babe in my womb leaped for joy'." (Luke 1: 41-44).

Unlike Elizabeth, her husband Zechariah was silenced and unable to speak for a season (Luke 1: 20) because of his unbelief when Gabriel announced to him that Elizabeth would conceive in her old age.

The story of "Naaman, the commander of the army of the king of Syria," is worth looking at (2 Kings 5). He was "a great man with his master and in high favor, because by him the Lord had given victory to Syria. He was a mighty man of valor, but he was a leper." Naaman had a big problem: he was a leper. A slave girl in his house told his wife about the prophet Elisha, who "would cure him of his leprosy." Naaman goes to see the prophet Elisha in order to get healed, and he almost didn't get healed because of his pride and arrogance. Naaman had his own idea of how he would get healed; he had it all planned out. However, when he got to the prophet's house, nothing turned out as he expected. Naaman became angry (v. 11) and even raged (v. 12). He wanted things his way; he wanted to be in control. Naaman was upset because the prophet didn't even come out to greet him! Elisha just sent a messenger to tell him what to do to get healed.

> "Go and wash in the Jordan seven times, and your flesh shall be restored, and you shall be clean." (v. 11).

What the prophet told Naaman to do just made him lose it! It was just too simple and foolish, it sounded so stupid; plus the rivers in Syria were much nicer than the Jordan! This is when he started raging. However, God in His mercy used his servants to put some sense into his mind:

> "My father, if the prophet had commanded you to do some great thing, would you not have done it? How much rather, then, when he says to you, wash, and be clean?" (v.13).

Naaman listened to his servants. He had to overcome his pride, arrogance, anger, rage, shame, fears and his controlling spirit; he had to become like a "babe!"

> "So he went down and dipped himself seven times in the Jordan, according to the word of the man of God; and his flesh was restored like the flesh of a little child, and he was clean."

"Trust in the Lord with all your heart, and do not rely on your own insight." (Proverbs 3: 3).

FORGIVE!

"And forgive us our debts, as we also have forgiven our debtors...." (Matthew 6:12).

This is "Christianity 101." This is basic Christian living for planet earth! Yet, I find so many that have not forgiven! Get over it, every person at one point or another is going to get hurt, rejected, abandoned, slandered, and the list goes on and on. Our response is what is important: we must forgive. It's not an option. Avail yourself of the grace of God to do what is humanly impossible for you to do. Remember, we "walk by faith" and by faith we lay hold of His grace to do what His Word tells us to do.

"And whenever you stand praying, forgive, if you have anything against any one; so that your Father also who is in heaven may forgive you your trespasses." (Mark 11:25-26).

The Word is very clear that we are forgiven as we forgive. As intercessors, unforgiveness will affect our "seeing" and our "hearing," because it's an open door for the enemy to harass us with confusion and spiritual blindness and deafness. Festering wounds will not heal until forgiveness takes place. Unforgiveness has many "family members": anger, resentment, bitterness; all of these give the enemy a legal right to torment us:

"Be angry but do not sin; do not let the sun go down on your anger, and give no opportunity to the devil." (Ephesians 4:26-27).

A good thing to do every night before going to bed, is to take an "inventory" of who you need to forgive, and then do it; we don't want the sun to "go down" being angry, bitter, resentful and full of unforgiveness. If we don't, we're giving opportunity to the devil to "steal, kill and destroy" in our lives. (John 10:10). In the parable of the unforgiving debtor (Matthew 18:23-34), Jesus says that when we refuse to forgive, our heavenly Father Himself will deliver us to the tormentors. That means that when we refuse to forgive, the enemy has a right to torment us. Torment us with what? Depression, fear, panic attacks, sickness of every kind. You name it!

My brother and I were praying for a beautiful young woman who was suffering from rheumatoid arthritis. She was miserable because of the pains in her body. The Holy Spirit revealed to us that she needed to forgive. We told her and she began to weep. She had had a disagreement with a classmate who was involved in santeria (Cuban voodoo); apparently her classmate did some kind of witchcraft as retaliation, as the arthritis developed after that incident. Once the young lady forgave, all the pain left! Thank you, Jesus!

As intercessors, we want to be as "clean" channels as possible. Forgiveness is non-negotiable!

"...as the Lord has forgiven you, so you also must forgive." (Colossians 3:13).

DON'T BOX THE HOLY SPIRIT!

"…and the Spirit of God was moving…." (Genesis 1:2).

Haven't you noticed that every battle in the Bible required a different strategy? Victory came as they obeyed the voice of the Lord. When it comes to intercession, why is it that we want to pray in the same way again and again and again? I believe we feel comfortable with the familiar. However, the Lord wants to take us out of our comfort zones! I believe this keeps us much more dependent on the Holy Spirit. The Holy Spirit is very creative and delights to partner with a people that are willing to see, listen and obey. I will share with you some of the different strategies in the Bible used by the Lord to win victories for His people.

As they came into the Promised Land, the Lord gave Joshua the strategy for taking Jericho, a very well fortified city. It involved marching around the city, the blowing of trumpets and a mighty shout. Then the walls came down. Didn't make any sense to the natural mind; but it worked! In the next city to be taken, Ai, they were surprised by defeat; sin was in the camp. However, after the sin was dealt with, the Lord gave Joshua the strategy. In this case, Israel had to pretend it was beaten and ambush the enemy, while all that time Joshua extended his javelin toward the city. Kind of strange, but it worked!

One of my favorites is found in 2 Chronicles 20. King Jehoshaphat faced three enemy armies more powerful than his. The strategy the Lord gave was to put the praisers at the head of the army. The king

"appointed those who were to sing to the Lord and praise him in holy array, as they went before the army, and say, 'Give thanks to the Lord, for His steadfast love endures for ever'." (2 Chronicles 20:21).

As they sang and praised the Lord, the Lord set an ambush in the enemy camp and they killed themselves off. Imagine what the Israelite army looked like! The praisers at the front of the army dressed in "holy array" and singing about the Lord's love! They must have looked like fools, but it worked!

When an army of a million men came against King Asa (2 Chronicles 14:9-12), all it took was a prayer that King Asa made to the Lord! In His desperation, the king cried out to the Lord and "the Lord defeated the Ethiopians before Asa and before Judah, and the Ethiopians fled." Why so easy? I don't have a clue.

King David had the habit of inquiring of the Lord before going into battle. As he obeyed the Lord, he moved in victory. In 2 Samuel 5 (v.23-25), the Philistines come against David. "And when David inquired of the Lord, He said,

> "You shall not go up; go around to their rear, and come upon them opposite the balsam trees. And when you hear the sound of marching in the tops of the balsam trees, then bestir yourself; for then the Lord has gone out before you to smite the army of the Philistines. And David did as the Lord commanded him, and smote the Philistines from Geba to Gezer."

As David followed the Lord's instructions, which were pretty specific, the Lord gave him the victory over the Philistines. The important thing is "to inquire of the Lord," listen, and obey. James says,

> "But be doers of the Word, and not hearers only, deceiving yourselves." (James 1:22).

The Holy Spirit is very creative and will show us how to intercede for each specific situation. We must be willing to follow the leading of the Holy Spirit as He shows us "invisible" things that we need to pray for or pray against.

I like the way the Lord gave Moses and His people victory in the battle against the Amalekites (Exodus 17). Moses told Joshua to fight Amalek, but he would "stand on the top of the hill with the rod of God in my hand."

> "So Joshua did as Moses told him, and fought with Amalek; and

Moses, Aaron, and Hur went up to the top of the hill. Whenever Moses held up his hand, Israel prevailed; and whenever he lowered his hand, Amalek prevailed. But Moses' hands grew weary; so they took a stone and put it under him, and he sat upon it and Aaron and Hur held up his hands, one on one side, and the other on the other side; so his hands were steady until the going down of the sun. And Joshua mowed down Amalek and his people with the edge of the sword."

Moses' posture with his hands raised up speak of intercession. Point of the story: as long as there was "intercession," there was victory. No intercession, no victory!

In 2 Kings 19, when King Hezekiah was faced with the threat of attack and defeat by the king of Assyria, he went before the Lord and spread out before Him the letter he had received from the enemy king:

"Hezekiah received the letter from the hand of the messengers, and read it; and Hezekiah went up to the house of the Lord, and spread it before the Lord. And Hezekiah prayed before the Lord...." (2 Kings 19: 14-15).

As Hezekiah humbled himself before the Lord and presented the enemy's letter, it was a prophetic act of intercession. He was acting out his complete trust in the God of Israel and placing the situation in His hands. There was a tremendous victory for Hezekiah and Judah as "the angel of the Lord went forth, and slew one hundred and eighty-five thousand in the camp of the Assyrians..." (2 Kings 19: 35). Imagine, such a huge portion of the enemy army wiped out, suddenly! The enemy king just departed and went back home!

Several years ago, as I was interceding for my two younger children, the Lord gave me a vision with a dance in it. The dance looked somewhat like an Indian battle dance. I understood by the Spirit that my "arrow" was that dance that He showed me. Every time I prayed for that particular intention, I would rise up and do the dance and thank the Lord for the victory. I had some friends join me in the dance; within a short time I experienced victory in that situation. Awesome God! I share this with you, because what the Lord shows us might look "foolish" to us, but as we respond in obedience to His revelation we will experience victory. That's the "arrow" that will hit the target.

The son of a sister in the Lord was suddenly taken into the intensive care unit of the hospital with great pain in his neck and back. As we were praying for him for healing in the prayer group, I saw an ugly, black hand gripping his head. I realized that the enemy was causing this pain. We proceeded in the Name of Jesus to take authority over the enemy and to command him to take his hand off this young man. We then prayed for his healing. From that moment on his pain did not get worse, and he started to progressively get well. Within three days he was out of the hospital. The pain was later diagnosed as meningitis. I mention this because not every time that a person has pain he or she will be set free with a simple prayer for healing; in this case we had to come against the enemy before praying for healing. We had to engage in paga's intercession. In Luke 13, Jesus was able to "diagnose" by the Spirit that the problem with the woman that was bent over and unable to stand straight, was a "spirit of infirmity." She had a physical problem, but the hidden cause was demonic. Jesus knew that satan had bound her. He spoke freedom to her:

> "Woman, you are freed from your infirmity." Then He laid hands on her, "and immediately she was made straight, and she praised God."

Jesus knew that before He could heal her He had to free her. I'm just trying to make the point that every case is different. However, the Holy Spirit has equipped us with supernatural, divine gifts to help us deal effectively and victoriously with every situation that we encounter. Amen!

One lady asked for prayer because she had been praying for healing for forty years and she had not been healed. I told her she needed to change the way she was praying. She was upset when I said that. Obviously, there was a hindrance somewhere preventing her from receiving her healing. I asked her how she was praying. Every time she prayed for healing, she added "if it's Your will." Well, that's not the prayer of faith. I know it sounds good, but that's the prayer of doubt! Faith must be released, as "without faith it is impossible to please Him (Hebrews11:6). Jesus already carried every sickness and disease on the Cross! (Isaiah 53: 4-5; Matthew 8:17). James says in Chapter 5:15:

"...and the prayer of faith will save the sick man, and the Lord will raise him up...." (James 5:15).

Beloved of the Lord, if you have been praying God's will for a long time, and have seen no results, please ask the Holy Spirit to show you what changes you need to make in your life and in your prayers!

"If any of you lacks wisdom, let him ask God who gives to all men generously and without reproaching, and it will be given him. But let him ask in faith, without doubting, for he who doubts is like a wave of the sea that is driven and tossed by the wind. For that person must not suppose that a double-minded man, unstable in all his ways, will receive anything from the Lord." (James 1:5-8).

PRAY IT THROUGH!

"Upon your walls, O Jerusalem, I have set watchmen; all the day and all the night they shall never be silent. You who put the Lord in remembrance, take no rest, and give Him no rest until He establishes Jerusalem and makes it a praise in the earth." (Isaiah 62:6).

In 2 Kings 13:14-19, there is the story of Joash, king of Israel who is in trouble and visits Elisha the prophet. King Joash runs to the prophet for help because the Syrians are attacking Israel. The prophet makes the king take a bow and shoot arrows, as a prophetic gesture of victory over the Syrians. In v. 17-19 the prophet tells the king:

"Open the window eastward; and he opened it. Then Elisha said shoot; and he shot. And he said, 'The Lord's arrow of victory, the arrow of victory over Syria! For you shall fight the Syrians until you have made an end of them.' And he said, 'take the arrows'; and he took them. And he said to the king of Israel, 'strike the ground with them'; and he struck three times, and stopped. Then the man of God was angry with him, and said, 'You should have struck five or six times; then you would have struck down Syria until you had made an end of it, but now you will strike down Syria only three times.'"

We should not limit the power of God, like King Joash did, but rather pray through until we see victory, until we see His will and purposes brought forth. King Joash stopped short of what God wanted him to do. He should have struck the ground until he sensed victory. When we fight the enemy, we need to keep "striking the ground" with our arrows until we defeat him. We need to keep the intercession flowing until we experience a release by the Holy Spirit. That's how our prayers hit the target and we start seeing results.

Jesus said that we "ought always to pray and not lose heart." (Luke 18:1). He commended the perseverance of a widow who "bothered" an unrighteous judge by continually going to him asking for vindication (Luke 18:1- 8). She would not give up! Think of this: one widow, with no one to help her, going against the system. She kept shooting her "arrows" until she experienced victory. The judge said,

> "Though I neither fear God nor regard man, yet because this widow bothers me, I will vindicate her, or she will wear me out by her continual coming." (v.4-5).

As we "bother" the Lord and cry out to Him "day and night," we will be vindicated! Look at what Jesus says:

> "Hear what the unrighteous judge says. And will not God vindicate his elect, who cry to Him day and night?" (v.7).

After Elijah's victory over the false prophets in Mount Carmel, he said "…there is a sound of the rushing of rain" (1 Kings 18:41). (The land had been in a drought for over three years at the word of Elijah because of their apostasy). The prophet

> "went up to the top of Carmel; and he bowed himself down upon the earth, and put his face between his knees. And he said to his servant, 'Go up now, look toward the sea.' And he went up and looked, and said, 'There is nothing.' And he said, 'Go again seven times.' And at the seventh time he said,' Behold, a little cloud like a man's hand is rising out of the sea.' And he said, 'Go up,' say to Ahab, 'Prepare your chariot and go down, lest the rain stop you.' And in a little while the heavens grew black with clouds and wind, and there was great rain."

On top of Carmel, the prophet "birthed" the promise of rain. He kept sending his servant to look and see if there was a cloud coming from the sea. Seven times the servant had to go and see; six times the answer was "no." The prophet kept pressing on and persevering until the seventh time, when the servant said that there was a cloud, the size of a "man's hand," coming out of the sea. Elijah interceded and did not stop until the little cloud appeared. What appeared as a little cloud, the size of a "man's hand," turned into "great rain." This is an awesome example of intercession; the prophet praying through and cooperating with God to bring forth His purposes. The number seven in the Bible is the number of completion; Elijah hit the target as he pressed on and his intercession became "complete". So don't give up if you've been praying God's will in a certain situation; keep pressing on until the intercession is complete. Victory is around the corner! It might start very small, the size of a "man's hand," but that's just the beginning! Keep shooting those arrows until you see victory!

After spending 15 years praying for my brother Rene's salvation, I got tired of seeing no results. On the contrary, as the years passed, he got deeper and deeper into New Age, following after gurus and Eastern religions. One day I told the Lord: "Lord, it's obvious that my prayers are not hitting the target. Could you please show me how to pray for my brother?" I prayed in tongues really hard, breaking through into the Spirit realm. The Lord showed me Lazarus' tomb (John 11), except that the stone had been removed from the cave. I sensed the Lord telling me to start praying prophetically for my brother. I started to speak out, commanding my brother to come out of the tomb: "Rene, come out of darkness into light; come out of death into life; Jesus is waiting for you. Jesus loves you and He waits for you. Come out! Jesus is waiting for you with open arms. Do not be afraid." Just as in the story of Lazarus, I prophetically gestured with a pair of scissors, loosing him from everything that was keeping him bound and blind. I prayed like this for months. His attitude towards us immediately changed and he started to spend more time with us. He started to show an interest in our faith in Jesus, something that he had previously detested. He started asking questions; we saw that indeed the Holy Spirit was drawing him to Jesus. I believe that our arrows were hitting the target. Our prayers for his salvation were fulfilled in front of our eyes, as he sat in a charismatic Mass in thanksgiving for my first book "There's Power in Your Tongue." The Holy Spirit came upon him and he started to speak in tongues; he was also set free from sexual addiction. Later he told me "For over 20 years I have been trying to set myself free from sexual addiction; what I couldn't do on my own the Holy Spirit did in three minutes." Alleluia!

"And I tell you, Ask, and it will be given to you; seek, and you will find; knock, and it will be opened to you. For every one who asks receives, and he who seeks finds, and to him who knocks it will be opened." (Luke 11:9-10).

I like the story of Joshua and the Israelites as they tried to take over the city of Ai (Joshua 8). The first time around they were surprised by defeat. In the second attempt the Lord gave them the strategy for victory. The Lord told Joshua to lay an ambush behind the city; to trick the inhabitants of Ai into pursuing them, thereby leaving the city unprotected. Then the Lord said to Joshua:

"Stretch out the javelin that is in your hand toward Ai; for I will give it into your hand." (Joshua 8:18).

As Joshua stretched out the javelin toward the city, "the ambush rose quickly out of their place, and as soon as he had stretched out his hand, they ran and entered the city and took it; and they made haste to set the city on fire." The Israelites were able to totally defeat the enemy,

"For Joshua did not draw back his hand, with which he stretched out the javelin, until he had utterly destroyed all the inhabitants of Ai." (v.26).

Joshua's attitude was totally different than King Joash's. Joshua was determined to win and persevered until he saw the victory; King Joash did not press on as he should and only gained partial victory. Let us not stop shooting arrows of victory, deliverance, healing and restoration through our proclamations and declarations until we see the victory. Remember, we have the power for life or for death in our tongues (Pro. 18:21).

"Your arrows are sharp in the heart of the king's enemies; the peoples fall under you." (Ps. 45:5).

DON'T THINK YOUR PRAYERS DON'T COUNT

"For everyone who asks receives...." (Matthew 7:8).

One of the biggest lies of the enemy is to make God's people think that their prayers are not important. This wrong and carnal thinking goes something like this: "I'm just one person, and the problem is too big. What good will my prayer do?" Thinking like this will keep you neutralized and ineffective for the Kingdom. I'm glad Abraham, Moses, Aaron, Esther, Daniel, (just to name a few) and even Jesus did not think like this! Proverbs 15:8b says,

"...but the prayer of the upright is His delight."

Consider Abraham, whom the Bible describes as "friend of God" (James 2:23). The Lord decided to share His plans regarding Sodom with His friend Abraham; Abraham's nephew, Lot, lived in Sodom.   As you know, the Lord does nothing without revealing His secret to his servants the prophets (Amos 3:7).

"The Lord said, 'Shall I hide from Abraham what I am about to do....'" (Genesis 18:17).

After the Lord speaks with Abraham, he

"...stood before the Lord. Then Abraham drew near, and said...."

This is key for intercession. We enter into the presence of the Lord and we STAND and we DRAW NEAR and we SAY. In other words, we enter His presence (through the Blood of Jesus), we stand on the solid rock of His Word, and we draw near to Almighty God to commune with Him. We say what is in our hearts, we plead with Him, until we get an answer.

Abraham pleaded with the Lord not to destroy Sodom. He appealed to His mercy. "Suppose there are fifty righteous within the city; wilt thou then destroy the place and not spare it for the fifty righteous who are in it?" (Genesis 18:24). As Abraham and the Lord conversed, Abraham realized there were not even fifty righteous in Sodom; not even 45; not even forty; not even thirty; not even twenty. Abraham stopped at ten. The Lord told Abraham, "For the sake of ten I will not destroy it." (v.32). However, there weren't even ten in Sodom! Sodom and Gomorrah were destroyed, but Lot and his family were rescued before the Lord rained fire and brimstone on the cities. I believe that if Abraham would have gone down to a lower figure, let's say five, or even one, the Lord would have spared the cities. The good news is that because of Abraham's intercession, the Lord sent angels to rescue Lot and his family.

> "So it was that, when God destroyed the cities of the valley, God remembered Abraham, and sent Lot out of the midst of the overthrow, when he overthrew the cities in which Lot dwelt." (Genesis 19:29).

It was because of Abraham that the Lord spared Lot! The Lord remembered His friend Abraham and intervened in order to save Lot and his family. Don't you give up as you stand in intercession for the lost! At the right time they will be delivered! Your prayers do make a difference!

The prophet Elijah was used mightily by the Lord at a very difficult time in Israel. The nation had backslidden and were worshipping false gods. The Lord used Elijah so powerfully that at Elijah's word the rain stopped for more than three years and at Elijah's word the rain came. Look at what James says about him:

> "Elijah was a man of like nature with ourselves...." (James 5:17).

I like that. James is saying that Elijah was just like us! But it's not about us! It's about Him working through us!

In the summer of 1999, a huge hurricane suddenly appeared on the scene. This hurricane was coming straight to Miami and it was bigger than Hurricane Andrew, which in 1992 devastated parts of Miami. The weathermen were describing this hurricane as the "monster" hurricane of the century. Four of us were gathered together praying and taking authority over this hurricane. I remember telling the Lord, "Lord, I'm a single mother and I don't have a clue nor the money to get my house ready. Like me there are many, plus all the old and sick people that can't help themselves. Mercy, Lord!" I started to pray in tongues and the Lord showed me a wall that was being built along the coast of Florida. I asked the Lord about it and He said that the wall "was the prayers of My saints." The sense that I got was that as God's people prayed against this hurricane, the wall kept building up. I shared this with my friends and we started to thank the Lord for His "wall" of protection and His mercy towards us. I had peace and I knew in my heart we would not be affected. As the hurricane came closer, it "suddenly" changed direction and started to head north without landing in Florida. The weathermen were saying something like "We don't understand it, but South Florida seems to have an invisible barrier." Well, we knew what had happened. God's people prayed and He answered our prayers. It was a good thing that God's people prayed! Thank you, Jesus!

On election day 2000, after having voted, three of us went to the Blessed Sacrament chapel to intercede for our nation. We realized the urgency of the moment; it would be a very close election. As believers, we stood behind George W. Bush because he stood for life. As we were interceding, I just started "claiming" the Cuban-American vote for Bush, since I'm Cuban-American. We then started "claiming" Florida for Bush. I believe that the Holy Spirit inspired us to pray that way, as later on Florida would be the decisive state! Not only does every vote count, but every prayer as well!

"The prayer of a righteous man has great power in its effects." (James 3:16).

BE SENSITIVE TO THE HOLY SPIRIT

"But you, beloved, build yourselves up on your most holy faith; Pray in the Holy Spirit...." (Jude 20).

Praying in the Holy Spirit, or tongues, gets us very fast into the Spirit realm. It's a tremendous gift of the Spirit. The "rivers of living water" (John 7:37-38) start to flow and we hear the voice of the Lord (Ps.29:3). We become sensitive to the promptings of the Holy Spirit. One Sunday afternoon, suddenly, I sensed the Holy Spirit telling me to get on my face and start praying. I immediately started praying in tongues, on the floor; I sensed an urgency in the Spirit. After praying for a while, I realized that I was praying for my children. I thought at first that was kind of strange because I had already prayed for my four children in the morning. I realized this was an emergency! Not understanding much, I kept praying in tongues and then I took authority over the enemy, forbidding him to touch my children. I asked the Lord to surround my children with an angelic protection from any evil attack, accidents, terrorism, sickness or disease. I started then to thank the Lord for what He was doing. I kept decreeing and declaring (out loud) God's protection over my children. I stopped when I sensed a release from the Spirit. Around 7:00 p.m. I received a phone call that my son Ricky was hospitalized in the trauma center of Jackson Memorial Hospital. He had been go-cart racing and had been hit from behind. The impact from the crash caused him to fly and land on his back, with the go-cart on top of him. He was rushed by helicopter to the trauma center, as he couldn't breathe. In faith I started to praise the Lord and thank Him when I got the news. I said "Lord, I believe Ricky is fine; that's why You had me on my face in prayer. Thank you for protecting my child." As I was getting ready to go to the hospital, I received another phone call telling me not to go to the hospital, as Ricky was being released. My son walked out of the hospital that same night, with pain in his ribs and bruises in his arm and leg, but alive! I'm so thankful to the Lord for sparing his life! (He has quit go-cart racing, thank you, Jesus!). By the grace of God I was sensitive to the Holy Spirit and responded to

His prompting. I believe that the Lord used my prayers to save my son's life. Isaiah 30: 21 says:

"And your ears shall hear a word behind you, saying, 'This is the way, walk in it....'"

A wonderful example of being sensitive to the Holy Spirit and responding to His voice is found in Simeon. The Holy Spirit had revealed to Simeon that he would not die until he saw the Messiah with his own eyes. On the day that Joseph and Mary took Jesus to the temple in Jerusalem, it says that Simeon

"...inspired by the Holy Spirit he came into the temple; and when the parents brought in the child Jesus, to do for him according to the custom of the law, he took him in his arms and blessed God and said "Lord, now lettest thou thy servant depart in peace, according to thy word; for mine eyes have seen thy salvation...." (Luke 2:27-30).

Talk about perfect timing! The same thing happened to Anna, the prophetess, a great intercessor, who

"did not depart from the temple, worshipping with fasting and prayer night and day. And coming up at that very hour she gave thanks to God...." (Luke 2:37-38).

Anna spent more than sixty years offering up prayers and intercession for the coming of Jesus. She got to see the reward of her prayers with her eyes. She never quit praying, for she knew the will of God and prayed it through until the promise was birthed.

My friend Ina was awakened by the Holy Spirit very early one morning, around 2:00. She immediately knew by the Spirit that she had to pray for her sons, not knowing exactly which one or why. She started to pray and woke up her husband and asked him to pray also. They both prayed, and after a while Ina sensed that it was for Carlos that they were praying for. It turned out that Carlos was "miraculously" saved from a horrible car accident in which the car next to him skidded and flew over the median without even touching Carlos' car. The other car hit a palm tree and the driver was killed. As Ina and her son talked about the accident the next day, they realized the Holy Spirit had awakened Ina moments before the accident took place. Ina's and her husband's prayers became arrows in the hand of God to protect their son Carlos in the midst of a horrible car accident. Thank you, Jesus!

BE SPECIFIC!

"And Jesus said to him, 'What do you want me to do for you?'" (Mark 10:51).

Imagine, Jesus asked blind Bartimaeus what he wanted from Him. Didn't Jesus know? Of course He did! In John 5, Jesus asked the man who was lame for 38 years "Do you want to be healed?" (v.6). At first glance it seems foolish that Jesus would ask such questions, when the answer was so evident. However, the Lord is interested in relationship and delights to see honesty and transparency in His people. Knowing our need and total dependence on Him will keep us humble.

In order to shoot our arrows and hit the target we must be specific. An archer doesn't just shoot arrows randomly, he shoots towards a specific place he wants to hit. He wants to hit the bull's-eye! The Scriptures are God's revealed will for our lives, which help us stay on track. The Holy Spirit is full of gifts that will enable us to pray effectively in order to hit the target. He will show us, for example, through the gift of discernment of spirits if the enemy is involved in a situation; a word of knowledge will help to unravel the situation to get to the root of the problem; a word of wisdom will show us what steps to take in order to bring the desired healing, deliverance, wholeness and restoration needed. The prophetic word can show us what the Lord's plans are for a certain situation or individual.

Years ago, when my son Eddy was a young teen, Catholic evangelist Greg Trainor prophesied over him a wonderful word from the Lord. Greg saw Eddy holding his Bible and people gathered around him, listening to his preaching. This word has helped me in part to know God's will for Eddy's life. This word I have prayed back to God again and again, and today at age 25 Eddy is still devoted to the Word of God. Thank you, Jesus! In a vision the Lord gave me about Eddy, I saw him as a doctor (he's in medical school) healing and taking care of the poor. I have prayed for my son that he would always have a heart for the poor and hurting. He has been going once a year with a team of Christian doctors to third world countries (Central America) to heal and pray for the sick. God is a faithful god! He delights to bless us as we pray and intercede for others, "far more abundantly than all that we ask or think...." (Ephesians 3:20).

After walking in the wilderness for forty years, God's people finally entered the Promise Land under the leadership of Joshua. Caleb was very specific about his inheritance: "Now therefore, give me this hill country...." (Joshua 14:12). His daughter had that same spirit. Caleb said to her,

"What do you wish? She answered, Give me a present; since you have set me in the land of the Negev, give me also springs of water. And Caleb gave her the upper springs and the lower springs." (Joshua 15:18-19).

This story about Caleb's daughter is also found in Judges 1:14. The Holy Spirit is trying to make a point; that it pleases God when we are bold to ask Him specifically the desires He has placed in our hearts. Let us not assume that He will do it without prayer and intercession! Let us not ignore this awesome privilege He has given to us His children of being able to boldly go before Him on behalf of others! Let us not assume that He will send the "rain" of the Spirit if we don't ask. The prophet Zechariah says in chapter 10:1:

"Ask rain from the Lord in the season of the spring rain, from the Lord who makes the storm clouds, who gives men showers of rain, to every one the vegetation in the field."

"O yes, 'Let us then with confidence draw near to the throne of grace....'" (Hebrews 4:16).

Another story worth mentioning is the story of the daughters of Zelophehad, because they too asked specifically for their inheritance. (This story is also found twice in the Bible). The four daughters come before Moses and the leaders of the tribes asking for land, as their father had died and had no sons. Therefore, there was no male heir to inherit the father's land. They said in Numbers 27: 4:

> "Why should the name of our father be taken away from his family, because he had no son? Give to us a possession among our father's brethren."

Moses took the case before the Lord, who said:

> "The daughters of Zelophedad are right; you shall give them possession of an inheritance among their father's brethren and cause the inheritance of their father to pass to them." (v.7).

These four ladies, Caleb, and Caleb's daughter dared to ask for what was rightly theirs. If they hadn't asked they would not have received what was theirs to begin with. In the same way, Jesus won for us an abundant life in Calvary; He won a promised life for us. There is an inheritance that is rightfully ours. We can either ignore it or start possessing what is ours. We can stand in the gap between God and others to intercede for what Jesus has already won for them in Calvary. It's our choice!

> "Therefore I tell you, whatever you ask in prayer, believe that you receive it, and you will." (Mark 11:24).

LAY DOWN YOUR LIFE!

"Arise, cry out in the night, at the beginning of the watches! Pour out your heart like water before the presence of the Lord! Lift your hands to Him for the lives of your children...." (Lamentations 2:19).

As God's people we need to be available and willing to be taken out of our comfort zones. We want to be docile to the promptings of the Holy Spirit and allow Him to change our plans. The Lord might start waking you up in the middle of the night to pray for someone; or He might tell you in the middle of the day to put everything aside and come into His presence; or He might just tell you to start praying in the Spirit. Many times suddenly, you will start thinking about someone you haven't thought about in a long time. Whenever and however He wants to use you, we need to be willing to follow the leading of the Holy Spirit. When we say "YES" to the Lord, He will take our "YES" very seriously and there will be great changes in us and through us.

In 2 Samuel 21, there's a very touching story about a woman named Rizpah, King Saul's concubine. David is king and there is a famine in the land. The famine is the result of King Saul killing the Gibeonites. The only way to put an end to this curse was by putting to death seven of Saul's descendants. Two of those that died were the sons of Rizpah.

"They were put to death in the first days of harvest, at the beginning of barley harvest. Then Rizpah the daughter of Aiah took sackcloth, and spread it for herself on the rock, from the beginning of harvest until rain fell upon them from the heavens; and she did not allow the birds of the air to come upon them by day, or the beasts of the field by night." (2 Samuel 21:9-10).

This is a story of intercession. I'm going to make it relevant for today. Rizpah, a mother, intercedes for her children, who are "dead" spiritually. She's determined to stand in the gap for them and through her prayers and intercession she builds a wall of protection around her children to keep the enemy (the birds and the beasts) away. Just as rotting flesh attracts the vultures or predators, the "spiritual stink" also attracts the enemy. She stood on "the rock" (Jesus Christ) interceding without ceasing, until "rain fell upon them…." She stood in the gap for her children until the rains of the Holy Spirit came upon them! This is exactly what we need to do for the "lost" children; intercede for them, keeping the enemy away and asking the Lord for the rains of the Holy Spirit to come down upon them, "For the promise is to you and to your children and to all that are far off, every one whom the Lord our God calls to Him." (Acts 2:39). Isaiah says,

> "For I will pour water on the thirsty land, and streams on the dry ground, I will pour My Spirit upon your descendants, and my blessing on your offspring." (Isaiah 44:3).

A beautiful example of a life laid down for God and His purposes is the prophetess Anna (mentioned in a previous chapter). She lived most of her life as a widow (over 60 years), and "she did not depart from the temple, worshiping with fasting and prayer night and day" (Luke 2: 37). She was widowed, but her life with the Lord blossomed. I believe she was a prayer warrior, interceding night and day for the coming of the Messiah. As a prophetess, she was totally focused on God in order to hear His voice. We know that she heard the voice of God, for on the day that Mary and Joseph took Jesus to the temple in Jerusalem, she came up "at that very hour." She got to see with her eyes the fruit of her intercession! For those "elderly" that might be reading this book, I tell you that there's no retirement in the kingdom! Look at Anna and be inspired!

My friend Marilyn Quirk, founder of "Magnificat, a Ministry to Catholic Women," has been used by the Lord mightily to intercede for His purposes. She has shared a very powerful story of intercession which really shows its power when the Holy Spirit initiates it. This is the story: together with her husband, Marilyn was at a huge Holy Spirit conference. Seated right in front of them was a couple; he seemed very angry and agitated at his wife for being there. Marilyn started to intercede for this man. That night, back at home, Marilyn could not sleep thinking about him. She got up and started to intercede for him; she spent hours weeping and travailing for him. The Lord showed her how to pray specifically; she "wrestled" with the enemy. When she felt a release by the Holy Spirit, she want back to bed, slept a few hours, and woke up refreshed the next morning. Back at the conference the next night, this couple is seated again in front of them! (That in itself was miraculous, as this was a huge conference of many thousands of people!). However, this time something was different. The man's demeanor was totally changed! He had his arms raised, praising God, and he was weeping! He looked like a new man! It seemed that he experienced a profound conversion to the Lord. The Lord showed Marilyn how powerful intercession can be when we allow the Holy Spirit to guide it! Marilyn's arrows hit the target! I think this is a beautiful example of a life laid down for the Lord. Marilyn spent hours in intercession for somebody she didn't even know! But this "somebody" was important to the Lord! Who knows how many tears the wife had shed for her husband's conversion; who knows how many years she had been praying for him? In the mystery of it all, Marilyn's prayers were needed for the Lord to answer the wife's prayers! My dear brothers and sisters, we have all been "strategically" placed by the Lord in the place we are. Let's open our eyes and ears and start allowing the Lord to use us in this mighty work of intercession, so that His plans and purposes can be accomplished according to His will. How willing are you to lay down your life to take up the work of intercession?

A very, very intense time of intercession took place in America on election day of 2000 and its aftermath. It plunged God's people to their knees! This was a battle between the forces of life and death; between light and darkness. My intercession most of the time took the form of weeping for this nation, repenting for the sins of our nation and asking God for mercy. Many believers experienced similar stories. There was a "laying down" of lives across America as the future of this country (and of the world) was at stake. The promise of 2 Chronicles 7:14 became more alive than ever:

" ...if my people who are called by My Name humble themselves, and pray and seek My Face, and turn from their wicked ways, then I will hear from heaven, and will forgive their sin and heal their land."

Our merciful God "heard" from heaven and the forces of life prevailed over the enemy.

A HEART FULL OF MERCY

"Go and learn what this means, I desire mercy...." (Matthew 9:13).

In order to intercede successfully, we need to have a heart like Jesus, who was full of compassion (Matthew 9:36). We can't be judgmental, critical or have the wrong motives. What we hear from the Lord, this is what we pray for. We identify with the people or the person we are interceding for. We don't want to be like Jonah! One way to "overcome evil with good" (Romans 12: 21) is to pray and intercede for our "enemies." This is one way we can fulfill Jesus' command to "love your enemies, do good to those who hate you, bless those who curse you, pray for those who abuse you" (Luke 6:27-28). At the Cross Jesus was interceding for us, the ones that nailed Him to it. Isaiah 53:12(b) says,

"...yet He bore the sin of many, and made intercession for the transgressors."

Luke records in chapter 23:34:

"And Jesus said, 'Father forgive them; for they know not what they do.'"

I still remember the day when the Lord broke my heart for the prostitutes. I ended up in the floor weeping and crying out to the Lord for mercy for these women! I really don't know how it happened, but I experienced the heart and the love of the Lord for these women. I was broken before the Lord for them; I kept asking the Lord to send workers of His vineyard to tell them about the love of Jesus! Years later, I was the answer to that prayer, as I've been going to the women's jail every Saturday, where many of the women are prostitutes. Thank you, Lord, for being able to labor with you!

In Exodus 32, when God's people turned to idolatry in the desert, the Lord was ready to get rid of them until Moses stood in the gap to intercede for them. The Lord even told Moses in v. 10 that He wanted to destroy them," but of you I will make a great nation." Moses interceded before the Lord and asked God to forgive their sin, "…and if not, blot me, I pray thee, out of thy book which thou hast written." (v.32). We get a glimpse of the heart of Moses; he was not interested in God making a great nation out of him. He just wanted the people he was leading to make it, to possess what God had promised them. He was so serious about it that he told God that if He didn't forgive them, might as well forget about him (Moses) too. How do you like that! Ps. 106:23 says:

> "Therefore He said He would destroy them had not Moses, His chosen one, stood in the breach before Him, to turn away His wrath from destroying them."

Moses' intercession was so effective that "the Lord repented of the evil which he thought to do to His people." (v.14). One person that had favor with God was able to save a nation! Doesn't this encourage you to make time to intercede for your family? If God was able to save a whole nation through one man's intercession, don't you think He will honor yours as you stand in the gap for your family? For the Church? For the nation?

The prophet Nehemiah was in exile and was grieved when he was told the condition of Jerusalem and its survivors. The survivors were "in great trouble and shame; the wall of Jerusalem is broken down, and its gates are destroyed by fire." (Nehemiah 1:3). What was his response?

"When I heard those words I sat down and wept, and mourned for days; and I continued fasting and praying before the God of heaven." (v.4). The Lord listened to Nehemiah's cry and used him to go back to Jerusalem to rebuild its walls, which were in ruins. Again, one man being used powerfully to fulfill God's purpose.

The Lord showed the prophet Amos several visions of His plans towards His people, and twice Amos was able to avert disaster. In the first vision, the Lord showed the prophet an invasion of locusts that would eat up the grass of the land. Amos cried out to the Lord and said

> "O Lord God, forgive, I beseech thee! How can Jacob stand? He is so small! The Lord repented concerning this; 'It shall not be,' said the Lord." (Amos 7:2-3)

In the second vision Amos saw that "the Lord God was calling for a judgment by fire, and it devoured the great deep and was eating up the land." The prophet said,

> "O Lord God, cease, I beseech thee! How can Jacob stand? He is so small! The Lord repented concerning this; 'This also shall not be,' said the Lord God." (Amos 7:4-6).

In spite of the persecution and rejection by the Jews, the Apostle Paul grieved in his heart for them. He suffered beatings, stonings, whippings, false accusations, imprisonments, at their hands. However, the fact that they rejected Christ kept Paul a broken man. He says in Romans 9:2-3:

> "...I have great sorrow and unceasing anguish in my heart. For I could wish that I myself were accursed and cut off from Christ for the sake of my brethren, my kinsmen by race."

Instead of being bitter, angry and resentful towards "his brethren," he experienced mercy and compassion for them. Only the grace of God can do such a supernatural work in a person's heart!

Often the Lord will show us through dreams and visions "negative" things, so that we pray against them, just like He did with the prophet Amos. Once the Lord gave me a dream of a friend in the Lord, who (in the dream) was telling me that she was going back to the world, as she was tired of following the Lord. I knew that the spirit of the world was really pulling my friend back into its grip. I experienced such a broken heart for her! Together with another friend, we agreed (Matthew 18:19) that this would not happen. We took authority over the enemy. We bound that spirit of the world in the name of Jesus and loosed our friend from it. We started to thank God for the plans He had for her and asked the Holy Spirit to hover over her and make Jesus more real than before. We cried out to God for mercy. My friend today is on fire for the Lord! Thank you, Jesus! She never went back to the "world." Amen!

In the summer of 2004, Miami was continuously being threatened with a series of hurricanes. One of them was Frances, who seemed to be coming directly to us. It was a category four (devastating) hurricane. Many believers were saying things like "Miami is such a sinful place; God is fed up with us; we deserve whatever comes our way...." I refused to think like that! I know that this city is full of sin and perversion, but I will always pray for mercy! "...mercy triumphs over judgment." (James 2:13). Once again, I started to cry out to the Lord on behalf of all the elderly, the sick, the poor, the single mothers who had no resources to get ready for the hurricane and their children (these are all dear to the heart of God!). This went on for several days. At one point I was praying with my brother over the phone for this hurricane to disintegrate; we started to pray in tongues. Suddenly, led by the Spirit, I started to speak directly to Frances: "Frances, I pluck out your "eye" and I trample over it with my feet." That's exactly what I started to do; my brother did it too. Can you believe that Frances lost her "eye", and remained on the same spot without moving for several days? Finally when she developed another eye, it was "wobbly" and not as powerful as the first one. The hurricane went down to a category two when it finally landed on the northwest coast of Florida. I wished that Frances would have disappeared altogether; however, I am thankful to the Lord for what He did. A category two hurricane is much, much better that a category four! Plus it didn't come to Miami!

Another area in which we can show mercy is with the poor and oppressed, the widows and orphans. The heart of God overflows with love and compassion for them. Recently I accompanied my friend Cristina to the bank. As we approached the bank, there was an elderly woman with a walker, right in the middle of the parking lot. She looked tired and weary; as if her ride had forgotten about her. Our hearts just broke with compassion for her. I went to her and told her we would take her home. Immediately she said: "The Lord must have sent you…." I helped her walk to the car and get inside the car; she had pain all over her hips and legs due to arthritis. On the way to her home, we started to praise the Lord and prayed for healing of her body. I cannot tell you how thankful she was; she kept saying "the Lord must have sent you!" As she got off, she realized that her body had much less pain and she could walk much, much better. There was such a presence of God in that random act of mercy! We sensed the Father's pleasure with us for having taken care of one of His children. Truly, it was a divine appointment!

"With what shall I come before the Lord, and bow myself before the High God? Shall I come before Him with burnt offerings, with calves a year old? Will the Lord be pleased with thousands of rams, ten thousands rivers of oil? Shall I give my firstborn for my transgression, the fruit of my body for the sin of my soul? He has shown you, O man, what is good; And what does the Lord require of you, but to do justly, to love mercy, and to walk humbly with your God?" (Micah 6:6-8).

A HEART FULL OF REPENTANCE

"The sacrifice acceptable to God is a broken spirit; a broken and contrite heart, O God, thou wilt not despise." (Psalm 51: 17).

Daniel was an exile in Babylon and he discovered by reading Jeremiah's prophecy that the specified time of exile was up. He did something about it: he turned to the Lord and he started to intercede to bring the promise to fulfillment. Daniel was a holy and upright man; however, he identified with and repented for the sin of his people. Daniel 9:3-5 says:

"Then I turned my face to the Lord God, seeking Him by prayer and supplications with fasting and sackcloth and ashes. I prayed to the Lord my God and made confession, saying...we have sinned and done wrong and acted wickedly and rebelled...."

Nehemiah, also an exile, identified with the sin of his people and turned to the Lord:

"....let thy ear be attentive, and thy eyes open, to hear the prayer of thy servant which I now pray before thee day and night for the people of Israel thy servants, confessing the sins of the people of Israel, which we have sinned against thee. Yea, I and my father's house have sinned. We have acted very corruptly against Thee...." (Nehemiah 1:6-7).

When Ezra the scribe was told that God's people "had not separated themselves from the peoples of the lands with their abominations" and had "taken some of their daughters to be wives for themselves and for their sons; so that the holy race has mixed itself with the peoples of the lands..." (Ezra 9: 1-2), this is how he responded:

"When I heard this, I rent my garments and my mantle, and pulled hair from my head and beard, and sat appalled.... And at the evening sacrifice I rose from my fasting, with my garments and my mantle rent, and fell upon my knees and spread out my hands to the Lord my God, saying: 'O my God, I am ashamed and blush to lift my face to thee, my God, for our iniquities have risen higher than our heads, and our guilt has mounted up to the heavens. From the days of our fathers to this day we have been in great guilt....'" (v.3-7).

Ezra was a broken man before the Lord for the sins of the nation! He totally identified with them and cried out to God for them. The Lord used him to make His people realize that they had to be separate from the nations surrounding them. They made a covenant with God and all that had married foreign women "put them away with their children." (Ezra 10:44).

We see these men burdened with the sin of their people; they were desperate! They turned to God with a broken heart, full of repentance. So many of us just criticize and pass judgement; let's change our criticism into intercession! We need to get desperate and turn to God instead!

Jesus so identified with us, that He not only bore our sin, but was made sin for us:

"For our sake He made Him to be sin who knew no sin, so that in Him we might become the righteousness of God." (2 Corinthians 5:21).

Let's approach His throne repenting, on behalf of our nation, our church, our family, our city in this time of need! Let our hearts break for the sins of our nation; let us cry out for the pain and brokenness, for the wounds and misery that surrounds our lives. We know the answer for every problem: JESUS! We know the only one that can satisfy: JESUS! We know the only one that can restore and make us whole: JESUS!

"Let us then with confidence draw near to the throne of grace, that we may receive mercy and find grace to help in time of need." (Hebrews 4:16).

A HEART FULL OF DESPERATION!

"Save me, O God! For the waters have come up to my neck. I sink in deep mire, where there is no foothold; I have come into deep waters, and the flood sweeps over me. I am weary with my crying; my throat is parched. My eyes grow dim with waiting for my God." (Psalm 69:1-3).

Who likes feeling like this? Who enjoys the "deep waters" of affliction and the "flood" of helplessness sweeping over our lives? Nobody enjoys desperation! But it is a very good thing when we turn to the Lord with it! Desperation is a grace from the Lord; It will drive us to Him. It means that He has opened our eyes so that we know we're very needy and dependent on Him; we're finally understanding reality! We know He's the only one that can help. Like Peter, we say,

"Lord, to whom shall we go? You have the words of eternal life; and we have believed, and have come to know, that You are the Holy One of Israel." (John 6:68-69).

In the Scriptures we see that the Lord Jesus always blessed those "desperate ones" that came to Him. The Canaanite woman that approached Jesus "interceding" for her daughter was one of those (Matthew 15:22-28). She had a good reason to be desperate: her daughter "was severely possessed by a demon." (v. 22).

She kept crying out to Jesus; it made His disciples very uncomfortable.

"And His disciples came and begged Him, saying, send her away…." (v. 23).

This woman was so desperate that she did not give up. (Please read the entire story).

No one could stop her from receiving! His disciples found her a pest; however, Jesus was touched by her determination to press on and persevere until she received what she came to get. Jesus answered her,

> "O woman, great is your faith! Be it done for you as you desire. And her daughter was healed instantly."

What an awesome story of intercession! The woman was so desperate that she didn't care what anybody thought of her. She refused to let anyone or anything stop her; she was completely focused and on target. Her "arrows" touched the Son of God!

Another desperate one is blind Bartimeaus (Mark 10:46-52). He also made people very uncomfortable as he shouted to Jesus for mercy.

> "They rebuked him, telling him to be silent; but he cried out all the more...."

Bartimeaus also didn't care what anyone thought of him. This was his chance: the Son of God was passing by as He was leaving Jericho. Bartimeaus thought "it's now or never!" Jesus blessed his desperation by healing him of blindness. Jesus said to him,

> "Go your way; your faith has made you well. And immediately he received his sight...." (v.22).

(Desperation makes people around us very uncomfortable, but it touches the heart of God! Jesus seems to love it!)

It was desperation for "bread" that made a friend go at midnight to a friend's house, asking for loaves to give to another friend (Luke 11:5-8). "Bread" stands for the word of God, as "Man shall not live by bread alone, but by every word that proceeds from the mouth of God." (Matthew 4:4). The friend said, "a friend of mine has arrived on a journey, and "I have nothing to set before him...." (v.6).

This is a good thing for us to know, the fact that we have nothing to "feed" anyone with, except what the Lord has given us. This is why the friend was so desperate! He needed a "word" for his friend! It was at midnight that he went asking for bread! He probably came shouting and probably woke up the neighbors! The other friend said "Do not bother me; the door is now shut...I cannot get up and give you anything?" (v.7), Jesus said,

> "I tell you, though he will not get up and give him anything because he is his friend, yet because of his importunity he will rise and give him whatever he needs." (v.8).

Yes, the friend's desperation for "bread," his persistence, made the other friend "uncomfortable"; he had to get up and give the friend what he was asking for. This is a beautiful story of intercession; we go before the "throne" (Hebrews 4:16) to ask for a "word" for a friend in need; wherever, whenever! And we keep knocking until we receive what we're asking for. Amen!

How about the desperation of the woman with the flow of blood (Mark 5:25-34); the desperation of Jairus asking Jesus for the healing for his daughter (Mark 5:22); the desperation of the centurion asking for the healing of his servant (Luke 7:2-10); the desperation of the official asking Jesus to heal his son (John 4:46-53); the desperation of the friends who broke through the roof so that Jesus could heal their friend (Mark 2:2-12); the desperation of the father wanting his epileptic son to be set free (Matthew 17:15-18)? All these people got blessed as they allowed their desperation to overcome every obstacle that stood between them and Jesus. Your level of desperation will determine what you receive from God!

> "If you then, who are evil, know how to give good gifts to your children, how much more will your Father in heaven give good things to those who ask Him!" (Matthew 7:11).

(A note on fasting. Fasting is a wonderful tool for intercession. It is really birthed out of desperation. Fasting helps to release revelation and to break the strongholds of the enemy. Look at Matthew 4:1; Acts 13:1-3; Esther 4:16; Daniel 9:3; Ezra 8:21; Isaiah 58; Jonah 3:5).

LOVE THE WORD OF GOD!

"Did not our hearts burn within us while He talked to us on the road, while He opened to us the scriptures?" (Luke 24: 33).

It takes the action of the Holy Spirit for us to desire and understand the Scriptures. In my own personal life, I never cared about the Scriptures. Even in those rare moments that I picked up a Bible, I couldn't understand it. However, when I gave my life to Jesus and was baptized in the Holy Spirit, suddenly I had an amazing desire to read God's Word. What was truly miraculous was that I could actually understand the Scriptures! The Holy Spirit opened my mind to understand the Scriptures, just as Jesus had done to His disciples just before His ascension (Luke 24:45). Truly, the Word of God became for me my daily bread. As the prophet Jeremiah says,

"Thy words were found, and I ate them, and thy words became to me a joy and the delight of my heart...." (Jeremiah 15: 16).

The Bible is our standard. It is full of promises for us, His people. "For all the promises of God find their Yes in Him (Jesus)" (2 Corinthians 1:20). If we don't know His promises, we cannot appropriate them. All prophetic revelation must be measured in the light of God's Word; this is why it's so important to study the Scriptures! The Holy Spirit, the author of the Bible, cannot contradict Himself. The Word of God is truth. We need to be rooted in the written Word before we can move well with "fresh" revelation from the Spirit. There seems to be a more accurate prophetic flow when the people have a solid foundation in the Scriptures, because our minds are renewed to think like He thinks and we know His heart.

Jesus, the Word made flesh, said:

"Every one then who hears these words of mine and does them

will be like a wise man who built his house upon the rock...and every one who hears these words of mine and does not do them will be like a foolish man who built his house upon the sand...." (Matthew 7: 24-27).

Our solid foundation is the Word of God; everything else is sinking sand!

"Forever, O Lord, thy word is firmly fixed in the heavens." (Psalm 119: 89).

"For You have magnified Your word above all Your name." (Psalm 138: 2). (NKJ).

"Heaven and earth will pass away, but my words will not pass away." (Luke 21:33).

Let me say again what Jesus did to His disciples just before His ascension,

"He opened their minds to understand the Scriptures...." (Luke 24: 45).

To intercede successfully we need to stand in His Word and remind Him of His promises, which are found in the Scriptures. Isaiah says,

"...You who put the Lord in remembrance, take no rest...." (Isaiah 62:6).

Moses reminded the Lord of His promise to the patriarchs as He was ready to get rid of the Israelites:

"Remember Abraham, Isaac, and Israel, thy servants, to whom thou didst swear by thine own self, and didst say to them, I will multiply your descendants as the stars of heaven, and all this land that I have promised I will give to your descendants, and they shall inherit it for ever. And the Lord repented of the evil which he thought to do to his people." (Exodus 32:14).

Nehemiah reminded God of His word (Nehemiah 1:8),

"Remember the word which thou didst command thy servant Moses...."

Daniel reminded God of His covenant and love (Daniel 9:4),

"...O Lord, the great and terrible God, who keeps covenant and steadfast love with those who love him and keep his commandments...."

Jesus Himself pointed to the Scriptures. When John the Baptist found himself in prison and was somewhat confused about Jesus (he was probably under attack!), he sent two of his disciples to ask Jesus "Are you he who is to come, or shall we look for another?" And Jesus answered them,

"Go and tell John what you hear and see: the blind receive their sight and the lame walk, lepers are cleansed and the deaf hear, and the dead are raised up, and the poor have good news preached to them." (Matthew 11:4-5).

Jesus was pointing John to Isaiah's prophecy concerning the Messiah (Isaiah 35:5-6 and Isaiah 61:1). Jesus was basically telling John the Baptist that what had already been prophesied concerning the Messiah by the prophet Isaiah was now being fulfilled in Him. Jesus was the fulfillment of that prophecy!

On Pentecost day, as people were "amazed and perplexed" (Acts 2:12), Peter had to clarify what was happening by pointing the people to Joel's prophecy (Joel 2:28-32). So we see how important the Scriptures are to keep us on God's track.

Having said that, however, the Apostle John says:

"Now Jesus did many other signs in the presence of the disciples which are not written in this book...." (John 20:30).

He also says,

"But there are also many other things which Jesus did; were every one of them to be written, I suppose that the world itself could not contain the books that would be written." (John 21: 25).

If we are confronted with something "new," check the fruit. We must exercise our discernment muscle! Pray and ask the Lord about it with someone more mature in the faith; "...in a multitude of counselors there is safety" (Proverbs 24: 6b). Prophetic revelation should be to upbuild, encourage and console. It's meant to edify the church. (1 Corinthians 14: 3-4). If it doesn't fit into this category and if the Lord is not being glorified through it, discard it. Don't let fear rule your life; allow the Holy Spirit, who is the Spirit of truth (John 15: 26), "teach you all things." (John 14: 26).

"The grass withers, the flower fades; but the word of Our God will stand forever." (Isaiah 40: 8).

LIVE IN THANKSGIVING AND PRAISE!

"Enter His gates with thanksgiving, and His courts with praise! Give thanks to Him, bless His name!" (Psalm 100: 4).

Only by the power of the Holy Spirit can we live lifestyles of thanksgiving and praise. In other words, because of the presence of the Holy Spirit, our lives overflow with a deep gratitude for what the Lord has done for us in Christ Jesus "with singing and making melody to the Lord with all your heart, always and for everything giving thanks..." (Ephesians 5:19-20). The Lord is looking for this kind of people, for such a time as this. We thank and praise Him because of who He is, not because of how we feel.

"Through Him then let us continually offer up a sacrifice of praise to God, that is, the fruit of lips that acknowledge His name." (Hebrews 13:15).

A key word here is "continually." We should be building "altars of thanksgiving" and "altars of praise" as we go through life on planet earth. We build those altars even if things are not going great. But He is great! That's why! Why is this important for us as intercessors? Because the Lord is "enthroned"on the praises of His people (Psalm 22:3). When we praise and thank Him, we position ourselves to hear His voice, because He shows up! Look at Psalm 84: 4-7:

"Blessed are those who dwell in thy house, ever singing thy praise! Blessed are the men whose strength is in thee, in whose heart are the highways to Zion. As they go through the Valley of Baca they make it a place of springs; the early rain also covers it with pools. They go from strength to strength; the God of gods will be seen in Zion."

Even when we go through the "valley of tears" we sing His praise, and that's how we make that place into "a place of springs." We turn it into a place of life, where the "rivers of living water" flow freely; the Holy Spirit strengthening us more and more. We know that the Lord inhabits our praises and the atmosphere changes as we praise Him. He shows up, His presence is manifested and great things happen. There we worship Him; He speaks to us, He heals us, He changes the way we think. We hear from Him. As intercessors, we receive revelation, insight, a vision, a word, right there in His presence.

I remember the day I took my eighty-year-old mother to one of her doctors. As she came out of the doctor's office, I could see mom was shaken. She had just received an unexpected negative report: her kidneys were functioning at a very low level and she might need dialysis. My mother was a doctor; doctors don't make very good patients! As we got in the car, I reminded her that there was another report:

"He took our infirmities and bore our diseases." (Matthew 8:17).

"By His wounds you have been healed." (1 Peter 2:24).

I told mom that this was the report that we believed! We started to move in thanksgiving for the healing of her kidneys; we sang His praises all the way home. The presence of the Lord was very strong; I had the "gut" feeling that the Lord was healing mom. I had one hand in the wheel and another hand on her back. We turned that place into a "place of springs," right there in my car! Dr. Jesus showed up, and His voice and His promise came with Him. Next time she went to the doctor, after some more tests, the doctor told her: "Your kidneys are okay; there's just like a little scar on the left one, but nothing to worry about." Thank you, Jesus!

Praise is also one of the biggest weapons we have against the enemy! Psalm 149:6 talks about the "high praises" of God in our mouths; those praises become like a sword that drives out the enemy! (Look at 2Chronicles 20):

"Let the high praises of God be in their throats and two-edged swords in their hands, to wreak vengeance on the nations and chastisement on the peoples, to bind their kings with chains and their nobles with fetters of iron, to execute on them the judgment written! This is glory for all His faithful ones." (vv.6-9).

In that atmosphere of high, exuberant praise, the enemy cannot stay. Wherever Jesus is lifted up, the enemy goes down! As intercessors, the "arrows" of praise should be flowing out of our mouths continually to stop the advancement of the enemy; "This is glory for all His faithful ones!" My friend's son was having a terrible time, full of self-pity and discouragement; he had been looking for a job for over a year and another door had just closed. My friend picked up her guitar and the high praises of God started to come out of her mouth. She felt the presence of God right there in her living room. The next day her son was free and hopeful once again. Thank you, Jesus!

"Therefore You will make them turn their back; You will make your arrows on Your string toward their faces." (Psalm 21:12). (NKJ).

III.
SHOOTING OUR ARROWS!

I will not dare put God in a box. I'm just sharing the "ingredients" of prophetic intercession. I am being honest with you in telling you, that every time I seriously intercede, it is always different! My best advice: feed on the Word of God and be led by the Holy Spirit, "who helps us in our weakness…" (Romans 8:26).

THE BLOOD OF JESUS: OUR VICTORY!

"And they have conquered him by the blood of the Lamb and by the word of their testimony...." (Revelation 12:11).

The blood of Jesus is our victory. We have to know this in order to conquer the enemy ourselves when he comes to attack each one of us individually with his lies and accusations. We cannot afford to be ignorant on this matter; if we are, we will not be able to resist because this is our victory and our protection over the enemy. We must have our testimony ready of what the blood of the lamb has done for us, because it's through the testifying of the power in the blood that it becomes effective in defeating the enemy. When the enemy comes to accuse and torment us, our weapon of victory is what the blood of Jesus has accomplished for us. As intercessors, this is vitally important, because our perspective totally changes. We stand on the finished work of Calvary. The triumph of the Cross is a done deal (Colossians 2:14-15). Through our intercession, we are basically enforcing what the Lord Jesus bought for us in Calvary. Let's look at what the blood of the Lamb has won for us:

- Because of the blood of Jesus we have forgiveness of sins. "Without the shedding of blood there is no forgiveness of sins." (Hebrews 9:22). One drop of the blood of Jesus is enough to take away the sin of the world! (It's because of His blood that the Sacrament of Reconciliation is so powerful!) When the enemy attacks you reminding you of your "sins," remind him of the Blood!

- Because of the blood of Jesus we have cleansing from all sin. "But if we walk in the light, as he is in the light, we have fellowship with one another, and the blood of Jesus his Son cleanses us from all sin." (1 John 1:7). The blood of Jesus is like a continual fountain of cleansing. When the enemy accuses you of your "latest" blunder, remind him of the Blood!

- Because of the blood of Jesus we have redemption. "In Him

we have redemption through His blood, the forgiveness of our trespasses...." (Ephesians 1:7). We have been bought back from the hand of the enemy; the price is the blood of Jesus! When the enemy reminds you of your past life, remind him of the Blood!

- Because of the blood of Jesus we have justification. "...Since all have sinned and fall short of the glory of God, they are justified by His grace as a gift, through the redemption which is in Christ Jesus, whom God put forward as an expiation by His blood...." (Romans 3:23-25). Justification is a legal term in which we are found not guilty, because of the blood of Jesus! When the enemy accuses you of guilt, remind him of the Blood!

- Because of the blood of Jesus we have sanctification. "So Jesus suffered outside the gate in order to sanctify the people through his own blood." (Hebrews 13:12). We have been set apart for God by the blood of Jesus! When the enemy tempts you with your old life, remind him of the Blood!

- We were ransomed by the blood of Jesus. "You know that you were ransomed from the futile ways inherited from your fathers, not with perishable things such as silver or gold, but with the precious blood of Christ, like that of a lamb without blemish or spot." (1 Peter 1:18-19). We don't belong to ourselves any longer; we belong to Him who bought us with His blood! When the enemy tries to make you feel like dirt, remind him of the Blood!

"But thanks be to God, who gives us the victory through our Lord Jesus Christ." (1 Corinthians 15: 57).

PUT ON YOUR ARMOR!

"Put on the whole armor of God, that you may be able to stand against the wiles of the devil." (Ephesians 6:11).

We are told to put on the armor of God, as spiritual warfare is part of our lives down here. We need to be protected, for we will come under attack. The enemy hates intercession. Therefore, before you enter into a time of intercession, make sure your armor is on securely (speak it out!). Every part of the armor protects an area of attack from the enemy, intended to cripple your walk and destiny in Christ Jesus by bringing confusion, doubts and deception. The armor is Jesus! Let's look briefly at each piece:

- "Having girded your loins with TRUTH." Jesus is the truth! (John 14:16). This belt protects a very sensitive area, the reproductive organs. We are supposed to reproduce as Christians by making disciples (Matthew 28: 19-20). The enemy wants us "barren."

- "Having put on the breastplate of righteousness" Jesus is our righteousness! (1 Corinthians 1:20). On our own we are "unclean, and all our righteous deeds are like a polluted garment." (Isaiah 64:6). His righteousness protects our heart, where faith and love reside (1 Thessalonians 5:8). As Christians, our "believing" is in the heart (Romans 10:9-10). The enemy attacks our faith, since "without faith it is impossible to please Him" (Hebrews 11:6). Love is our motivation; what matters is "faith working through love" (Galatians 5:6). The enemy attacks to stop our motivation and be rendered ineffective for Kingdom purposes.

- "Having shod your feet with the equipment of the gospel of peace;" Jesus is my "Prince of Peace" (Isaiah 9:6). We are "ambassadors for Christ" (2 Corinthians 5:20), on the move, with "the ministry of reconciliation" (2 Corinthians 5:18). We carry the "good news" of reconciliation, letting people know that there is forgiveness available in Christ Jesus. We need to be ready, "with our shoes on," to go wherever He sends us to proclaim the gospel of peace. The enemy loves to steal those shoes, so that we don't go!

- "Above all taking the shield of faith, with which you can quench all the flaming darts of the evil one." Jesus is my shield! (Psalm 18: 2). What are the "flaming darts of the evil one?" They are the lies, deceptions, and temptations that he sends our way in order to make us doubt and waver in our faith. That's why feeding on the Word of God is vitally important, because faith comes by hearing, hearing by the Word of God (Romans 10:17). We must have renewed minds! The enemy wants us neutralized and paralyzed through his lies and deceptions.

- "And take the helmet of salvation." Jesus is my Savior! (Luke 2:11). This helmet protects my mind, the center of the warfare. I need to know that my salvation is not a nice idea or thought, but a fact and a reality. The blood of Jesus has done it all! I know I am a child of God! My thought life is centered on Jesus and His Word. The enemy comes with worldly thoughts, confusion and doubt to keep us from advancing.

- "And the Sword of the Spirit, which is the Word of God." Jesus is the Word! (John 1:1). This is the offensive weapon of the armor: the Word of God quickened by the Holy Spirit. When we wield this weapon, the enemy has to flee; just like with Jesus in the desert (Matthew 4:1-11). As we speak out the Word of God (this is not a mental exercise!), we take the offensive against the enemy. We resist him and he has to flee (James 4:7).

- "Pray at all times in the Spirit, with all prayer and supplication." The gift of tongues is particularly helpful for prayer; we can use it anytime! Prayer is simply communicating with the Lord; don't complicate it! There will be tons of good excuses for not praying; don't give in to them!

"Let the redeemed of the Lord say so, whom He has redeemed out of the hand of the enemy." (Psalm 107:2). (NKJ).

FOCUS AND AIM YOUR "ARROWS!"

"...keep alert with all perseverance, making supplication for all the saints, and also for me, that utterance may be given me in opening my mouth boldly to proclaim the mystery of the gospel...." (Ephesians 6:18-19).

In order to shoot our arrows, our focus must be clear. We want to hit the target; we want to hit bull's-eye! What is the burden in your heart? What has the Lord deposited in your heart that you know He wants you to pray for? We want to advance the Kingdom of God, we want "His kingdom to come, and His will be done on earth as it is in heaven" through our intercession. We need to know what we're aiming at. The desires of His heart are what we want to see realized. First of all, these are some areas that we can target (by no means a complete list):

- People in "high" places of authority: presidents, kings, governors, elected officials, head of corporations and universities, educators, etc., so "that we may lead a quiet and peaceable life, godly and respectful in every way" (1 Timothy 2:1-2). We pray for their conversion to Christ!

- For the proclamation of the Gospel, since "it is the power of God for salvation." (Romans 1:16), and the Lord "desires all men to be saved...." (1 Timothy 2:3). We pray for more workers of the vineyard to be released in the nations, governments, marketplaces, schools, hospitals, etc., to boldly proclaim and show the power of the Gospel of the Kingdom. We pray for signs and wonders to confirm the word preached. We pray for the lost, for the Holy Spirit to start softening their hearts and opening their ears to receive the seed of the Word of God.

- For the Church (us), that we would be a "house of prayer for all the nations" (Mark 11:17); a people that seek His face continually and that we would rise up in the power of the Holy Spirit to carry on with "the works of Jesus." (John 14:12). We pray for wisdom, revelation, boldness for our Pope and bishops; we pray for seminaries that they will truly be holy ground in which priests are set on fire for Jesus; we pray for revival!

- For justice in the courts, that the Lord will raise up a generation of judges and lawyers that will promote equity and justice for all. "For the Lord loves justice; He will not forsake His saints." (Psalm 37: 28). "Open your mouth for the dumb, for the rights of all who are left desolate. Open your mouth, judge righteously, maintain the rights of the poor and needy." (Proverbs 31:8-9).

- For mercy for the poor, orphans, widows; they hold a very special place in the heart of God! "The lord watches over the sojourners, he upholds the widow and the fatherless...." (Psalm 146:9). "Religion that is pure and undefiled before God and the Father is this: to visit orphans and widows in their affliction...." (James 1:27). "Cursed be he who perverts the justice due to the sojourner, the fatherless, and the widow." (Deuteronomy 27:19).

- For unity in the Body of Christ. Jesus prayed in John 17 five times for the unity of His people. When there's unity in His body, this is when the world will believe (John 17:23). Division in His Body is not only a scandal, but the devil's strategy to keep us from advancing, for a house divided cannot stand (Matthew 12:25). The Lord has commanded blessing when we "dwell in unity." (Psalm 133).

- For life "from the womb to the tomb." "...My frame was not hidden from thee, when I was being made in secret, intricately wrought in the depths of the earth. Thy eyes beheld my unformed substance; in thy book were written, every one of them, the days that were formed for me...." (Psalm 139:15-16). The Lord is the giver of life; He alone can take it! We pray for an end to abortion, euthanasia and all the research going on trying to manipulate life.

- For the peace of Jerusalem! This is dear to the heart of God. The Jews are the "apple of His eye!" (Zechariah 2:8). True peace can come only as they turn to the Lord Jesus Christ. Pray for massive conversion to Jesus and protection from their enemies. "Pray for the peace of Jerusalem! May they prosper who love you! Peace be within your walls, and security within your towers!" (Psalm 122:6-7). Let's pray for the continued support of Israel (Genesis 12:2-3).

- For the entertainment industry, that it would become a "God-fearing" industry as the Holy Spirit brings it under conviction of sin. (John 16:8-11). We pray for a reversal of all the moral filth and corruption coming out of this industry.

- For an end to terrorism; we ask the Holy Spirit to reveal the hidden strategies and plans of destruction. More than that, we pray that "God may perhaps grant that they will repent and come to know the truth, and they may escape from the snare of the devil...." (2 Timothy 2:25-26).

- Restoration of families. What family has not been touched by separation, division, divorce, addictions, anger, unforgiveness, resentment, disappointments of every kind? "They shall build up the ancient ruins, they shall raise up the former devastations; they shall repair the ruined cities, the devastations of many generations." (Isaiah 61:4).

"...the kingdom of heaven has suffered violence, and men of violence take it by force." (Matthew 11:12).

REPENT!

"Woe to you, Chorazin! Woe to you, Bethsaida! For if the mighty works done in you had been done in Tyre and Sidon, they would have repented long ago, sitting in sackcloth and ashes." (Luke 10:13).

I have shown how God's people repented for the sins of their nation. They identified with their people; they were desperate and broken; burdened with the sin and that's how they came before God pleading for mercy. They didn't have a "holier-than-thou" attitude. All of us are responsible for the state of the church and nation. Strongholds of sin bring curses upon the land. Some of the things we can repent for (this is not a complete list):

- Idolatry and greed. The Apostle Paul calls greed idolatry (Colossians 3:5). We can say that America today is an idolatrous nation. In 1 Timothy 6:10 he says "the love of money is the root of all evils...." Not only is greed a form of idolatry, but it also opens the door to "all kinds of evil!"

- Witchcraft, false religions, New Age, psychic hotlines, occultism, horoscopes, etc. All of these mentioned (and more!) are on the increase. Psychic hotlines are a multi-million dollars business! One reason for this is that people have not seen the power of God in the Church, so they go elsewhere for it. "There shall not be found among you... any one who practices divination, a soothsayer, or an augur, or a sorcerer, or a charmer, or a medium, or a wizard, or a necromancer. For whoever does these things is an abomination to the Lord...." (Deuteronomy 18:10-12).

- Sexual immorality: fornication, homosexuality, adultery, pornography. There has been an erosion of moral values; however, His standards remain the same! (1 Corinthians 6:9-10). (Exodus 20:15).

- Pride and independence from God. "...For my people have committed two evils; they have forsaken me, the fountain of living waters, and hewed out cisterns for themselves, broken cisterns, that can hold no water." (Jeremiah 2:13). "...They are darkened in their understanding, alienated from the life of God because of the ignorance that is in them, due to their hardness of heart; they have become callous and have given themselves up to licentiousness, greedy to practice every kind of uncleanness." (Ephesians 4:18-19).

- Lukewarmness, complacency, favoritism, prayerlessness in the Church. "So because you are lukewarm, and neither cold nor hot, I will spew you out of my mouth." (Revelation 3:16). "My brethren, show no partiality as you hold the faith of our Lord Jesus Christ, the Lord of glory." (James 2:1).

- Generational curses and sin in the region where we live. Just as we individually have a family tree that reveals sin and the root of curses in our families, there is a history behind the cities and regions where we live. "Like a sparrow in its flitting, like a swallow in its flying, a curse that is causeless does not alight." (Proverbs 26:2). These curses can be broken through repentance and standing on the Word of God. Galatians 3:13-14 says "Christ has redeemed us from the curse of the law, having become a curse for us—for it is written, 'Cursed be every one who hangs on a tree'—that in Christ Jesus the blessing of Abraham might come upon the Gentiles, that we might receive the promise of the Spirit through faith." As long as the curses remain, the enemy has a "legal right" to attack!

- Murder, rape, abuse, violence, abortion. "You shall not kill." (Exodus 20:13). "You have heard that it was said the men of old, You shall not kill; and whoever kills shall be liable to judgment. But I say to you that every one who is angry with his brother shall be liable to judgment; whoever insults his brother shall be liable to the council, and whoever says, 'You fool!' shall be liable to the hell of fire." (Matthew 5:20-22).

- Addictions to drugs and alcohol. This epidemic of drugs and alcohol abuse is connected to witchcraft! The word for drugs in Greek is the same word used for sorcery: "pharmakeus." You know who's behind it!

- Racism. "And He made from one every nation of men to live on all the face of the earth...." (Acts 17:26). "You shall love your neighbor as yourself." (Matthew 22:39).

"Hate evil, and love good, and establish justice in the gate; it may be that the Lord, the God of hosts, will be gracious to the remnant of Joseph." (Amos 5:15-16).

REMIND HIM OF HIS PROMISES!

"Upon your walls, O Jerusalem, I have set watchmen; all the day and all the night they shall never be silent. You who put the Lord in remembrance, take no rest, and give Him no rest until He establishes Jerusalem and makes it a praise in the earth." (Isaiah 62:6-7).

There are thousands of promises in the Scriptures for us; and there are personal promises that the Lord might have given you. We can remind Him of all of them! The exhortation here is not to give up, but to keep "reminding" Him. He responds to His Word. We have seen how the saints in the Bible stood on His Word and promises and persevered in prayer and intercession until they received the answer. The Lord is faithful to His Word, He is not a liar:

"God is not man, that He should lie, or a son of man, that He should repent. Has He said, and will He not do it? Or has He spoken, and will he not fulfill it?" (Numbers 23:19).

For every area that we repent for, there is a promise of restoration. What promises has He given you? Have you seen them all fulfilled, or are there some that still need fulfillment?

A friend of mine, a single mother, underwent surgery and something very unexpected took place. She says that in the middle of surgery she died; she saw her spirit leave her body and she encountered Jesus. She started to plead with the Lord telling Him that she didn't want to die; she had a daughter that needed her. Jesus showed no emotion at her appeal. However, when she "reminded" the Lord of His promises to her that were still unfulfilled, immediately she went back to her body. I think this is an amazing story; it really shows how committed the Lord is to His Word!

"...for I am watching over My word to perform it." (Jeremiah 1:12).

THANK and PRAISE HIM! WORSHIP HIM!

"O give thanks to the Lord, for He is good; His steadfast love endures for ever! Let Israel say, His steadfast love endures for ever." (Psalm 118:1-2).

We move in thanksgiving and praise! We are a tribe of worshipers!

"I will praise the name of God with a song; I will magnify Him with Thanksgiving. This will please the Lord more than an ox or a bull with horns and hoofs." (Psalm 69:30-31).

Be led by the Holy Spirit. Don't be in a rush! Allow Him to lead. Take time to thank and praise Him; let the "high praises" of God come out your mouths (Psalm 149:6). Pray in the Spirit and press on; sing in the Spirit; make "new" sounds as you hear the sounds of heaven. Move your body; dance, twirl, spin; be free! (2 Corinthians 3:17).

Worship Him when you experience His presence. Be intimate with Him. Enjoy being with Him. There's a relationship between worship and warfare, because in His presence:

"There is fullness of joy" (Psalm 16:11).

and

"The joy of the Lord is your strength" (Nehemiah 8:10).

In His presence we are strengthened for battle. He will guide you by speaking to you. He might give you a vision or a sense. He might show you the enemy at work. He might give you a song or a passage of Scripture. Later on He might give you a dream while you sleep. Don't be surprised if He tells you something that you were not expecting! It might not make a lot of sense to you, but it's important for Him! He's sharing His heart with you!

During this time, let the gifts of the Holy Spirit flow. Speaking or singing in tongues creates an atmosphere in which the gifts start to flow. The prophetic word or song, a vision, word of knowledge, word of wisdom, interpretation of tongues, discernment of spirits, will become "arrows" as we proclaim and declare what the Lord is showing us.

"For thus says the Lord: Sing aloud with gladness for Jacob, and raise shouts for the chief of the nations; proclaim, give praise, and say, the Lord has saved his people, the remnant of Israel." (Jeremiah 31:7).

SHOOT YOUR ARROWS: PROCLAIM, DE-CLARE, DECREE, ACT OUT!

"...Who confirms the word of His servant, and performs the counsel of His messengers; who says of Jerusalem, 'She shall be inhabited,' and of the cities of Judah, 'They shall be built, and I will raise up her ruins.'" (Isaiah 44: 26).

Whatever the Lord speaks or shows you, as you believe it and then proclaim and declare it (or act out), that becomes your "arrow." Release your faith by using your mouth to do so. There is power in your tongue! (Proverbs 18:21). He says that He is "watching over my word to perform it." (Jeremiah 1:12). The prophet Elisha said to King Joash:

"The Lord's arrow of victory, the arrow of victory over Syria! For you shall fight the Syrians in Aphek until you have made an end of them. And he said, 'Take the arrows'; and he took them. And he said to the king of Israel, 'Strike the ground with them'; And he struck three times, and stopped. Then the man of God was angry with him, and said you should have struck five or six times...." (2 Kings 13: 18-19).

Don't stop shooting those arrows of victory and deliverance until you see the enemy defeated! Don't be like King Joash, who stopped short and received only partial victory! The prophet got angry at him because he didn't have enough vision to keep pressing on to victory. Let's not limit God by our lack of vision!

I like how "The Message," *The Bible in Contemporary Language*, interprets Proverbs 29:18:

"If people can't see what God is doing, they stumble all over themselves; but when they attend to what He reveals, they are most blessed."

Obviously, King Joash stumbled because he didn't see what

God was doing; but we have a Helper that lives within us! Let's ask the Holy Spirit to help us "attend to what He reveals," so that we can be effectively used by God to fill the earth "with the glory of the Lord" (Numbers 14:21). I don't want partial victory, do you? No, we press on in the Spirit until His victory is complete! Amen.

"Likewise the Spirit helps us in our weakness; for we do not know how to pray as we ought, but the Spirit Himself intercedes for us with sighs too deep for words. And He who searches the hearts of men knows what is the mind of the Spirit, because the Spirit intercedes for the saints according to the will of God." (Romans 8:26-28).

WE BECOME HIS ARROWS!

"You will also declare a thing, and it will be established for you." (Job 22:28). (NKJ).

I believe the Lord wants every one of His children to be turned into prayer warriors and intercessors. That's one of the reasons He allows difficulties and trials in our lives. Yes, it's in that hard place that He trains us for battle (Psalm 144:1). Remember, He waits for us to ask. We limit Him when we don't pray! Every difficulty and trial that comes our way is an opportunity to exercise our privilege as priests and kings (1 Peter 2:9) to change things around and see His glory released. The Lord says in Zechariah 9:12b:

"Even today I declare that I will restore double to you." (NKJ).

He has "blessed us in Christ with every spiritual blessing in the heavenly places...." (Ephesians 1:3). He has gifted us with the gifts of His Holy Spirit (1 Corinthians 12:8-10). We lack nothing! The Lord is training us for greater things! He wants us to increase in His authority. "He who conquers, I will grant him to sit with me on my throne...." (Revelation 3:21). As we respond to the call to intercession, we will start being better listeners and seers and more sensitive to the Holy Spirit. The Lord is looking for a people that will pray His prayers to birth His purposes and extend His kingdom. The victory is ours! The enemy is a defeated foe! (Colossians 2:14-15).

And He taught, and said to them,

"Is it not written, My house shall be called a house of prayer for all the nations?" (Mark 11:17).

We are to show the world the character of Jesus as we live and walk in the Spirit (Galatians 5:25). We are to "spread the fragrance of the knowledge of Him everywhere. For we are the aroma of Christ...." (2 Corinthians 2:14-15). One thing the Lord has shown

me, especially in difficult moments, is to "stay" within the bound-
aries of the fruit of the Holy Spirit (Galatians 5:22-23). We are
to look like Him, who is "kind to the ungrateful and the selfish"
(Luke 6:35). Instead of reacting in the flesh, let us respond in the
Spirit, overcoming evil with good (Romans 12:21). As intercessors, we should look for opportunities to live out our intercession.
For example, in an area of greed and materialism, let us practice
generosity; in an area where anger and hatred abounds, let us release
love and kindness; in an area of strife and contention, let us walk
in the peace of the Lord. As we do so, a shifting in the spiritual
realm will start to take place. In this way, we become *"An Arrow
in His Hand."*

Dear reader, my prayer is that there's a fire burning in your
heart for more of God. As you seek His face, He will reward your
efforts (Hebrews 11:6b). It's His desire to draw you close and
reveal His heart to you. It's His desire to change you into a "first
class warrior!" Your prayers of intercession are important! I pray
that they rise before Him as sweet incense in His sight! It doesn't
matter who you are, how old or how young, the color of your skin,
what you do in life…. He's waiting for you to approach Him. As
you hear, believe and proclaim, you will see His power and glory
released! Amen!

"The glory of Lebanon shall come to you, the cypress, the
plane, and the pine, to beautify the place of My sanctuary; and
I will make the place of My feet glorious. The sons of those
who oppressed you shall come bending low to you; and all
who despised you shall bow down at your feet; they shall call
you the city of the Lord, the Zion of the Holy One of Israel."
(Isaiah 60:13-14).

Maria Vadia

"Heavenly Father, I come before you this day with a repentant heart.

Lord Jesus, I believe You are the Son of God; I believe that You died for me on the Cross of Calvary and paid the penalty for all my sins.

Please forgive me.

Wash me clean with your precious blood.

I confess with my mouth what I believe in my heart, that Jesus is Lord and that God raised Him from the dead.

I place my trust for my salvation upon Your finished work of the Cross.

Thank you, Lord, for the gift of salvation and eternal life."